D1799935
9780345026071

Lidice: sacrificial village

John Bradley

BB

Editor-in-Chief: Barrie Pitt
Editor: David Mason
Art Director: Sarah Kingham
Picture Editor: Robert Hunt
Consultant Art Editor: Denis Piper
Designer: David A Evans
Illustration: John Batchelor
Photographic Research: Jonathan Moore
Cartographer: Richard Natkiel

Photographs for this book were especially selected from the following Archives: from left to right page 2-3 Imperial War Museum; 7 Czechoslovak News Agency Photo Service; 8-9 Czech News Agency; 10-11 Keystone News Agency; 12 Czech News Agency; 13-15 US National Archives; 16 Czech News Agency; 18 US Archives; 19 Radio Times Hulton Picture Library; 20 US Archives; 21 Czech News Agency; 22-23 RTH; 22-23 Czech News Agency; 25 Czech News Agency; 26-27 US Archives; 28 Staatsbibliothek, Berlin; 28-29 Bundesarchiv, Koblenz; 30-32 Czech News Agency; 34-35 Pictorial Press; 36 Ullstein GmbH, Berlin; 37 Czech News Agency; 38-39 Staatsbibliothek; 40-41 Czech News Agency; 43 US Archives; 44-45 Staatsbibliothek; 46-47 Czech News Agency; 48-49 Pictorial Press; 50 IWM; 51 Staatsbibliothek; 56-57 Czech News Agency; 58-59 Staatsbibliothek; 60-62 Czech News Agency; 62 Bundesarchiv; 63-65 Czech News Agency; 66 Rijksinstituut, Amsterdam; 67 Czech News Agency; 68-69 Bundesarchiv; 70-71 Czech News Agency; 72-73 US Archives; 76-77 Czech News Agency; 78 Ullstein; 78-83 Czech News Agency; 84-85 Ullstein; 87-89 US Archives; 91-93 Czech News Agency; 94-95 Ullstein; 96-98 Czech News Agency; 99-101 Ullstein; 102-103 Czech News Agency; 105 Ullstein; 106-110 Czech News Agency; 112-113 IWM; 114 Czech News Agency; 115 Bundesarchiv; 116-125 Czech News Agency; 126-127 Staatsbibliothek; 128-129 IWM; 130-135 Czech News Agency; 136 US Archives; 137 Czech News Agency; 137 Black Star Publishing Ltd; 138 Keystone; 140 Ullstein; 141 Czech News Agency; 142-143 US Archives; 144-145 Czech News Agency; 146 US Archives; 150-153 Czech News Agency; 154-155 Ullstein; 156-159 US Archives; Front cover: Czech News Agency; Back cover: Bundesarchiv.

First Printing: August 1972
Printed in United States of America

Ballantine Books Inc.
101 Fifth Avenue New York NY 10003

An Intext Publisher

Contents

The tragedy of Lidice

Introduction by S L Mayer

Czechoslovakia has had a particularly unhappy history in the Twentieth Century. Indeed, although Czech nationalism has been extant for centuries (Jan Hus was a champion of Bohemian separatism in the 15th century) the fate of Czechoslovakia in recent times has been little better than that of Hus, their martyred hero, who was burned at the stake in 1415. Within the space of thirty years the Czech state, a child of the 20th century, created out of the chaos of the disintegrating Austro-Hungarian Empire at the end of the First World War, has been left alone to face the wrath of her more powerful neighbours. In 1938 the Munich Conference decided on the partition of Czechoslovakia, and within six months of that infamous pact, Czechoslovakia, as Hitler so succinctly put it, had 'ceased to exist'. Reconstructed after the war, Czechoslovakia again fell under the hands of external force, this time exerted by the Soviet Union, in 1948. And in 1968, fearful of Dubcek's brand of liberal socialism, Russia sent her tanks in to occupy Czechoslovakia and thereby awakened echos of the Cold War. Benes, the Premier of Czechoslovakia during both the 1938 and 1948 crises, remarked before his death that at least Bohemia and Moravia had been spared most of the agonies of war, and that Prague, the Golden City, had been left intact while her other Central and Eastern European neighbouring capitals, like Berlin and Budapest, had either been razed to the ground or torn to pieces by fierce fighting during the Second World War. Of course, to an extent this was true. But this is not to say that Czechoslovakia was spared from other, no less poignant tragedies.

In 1942 the town of Lidice was unknown. It was a village, like thousands

of others, sleepingly living through its daily life, untouched by the storms which swept through much of Europe. Its rude awakening put Lidice on the map of the world so that its name today, like that of Guernica in Spain, and Auschwitz in Poland, is remembered for the horrors, brought on by war, which took place there. When Reinhard Heydrich, Protector of Bohemia, was murdered, the vengeance of Nazism was carried out on this unknown village. Its citizens were slaughtered to a man, and, like ancient Carthage, its soil was salted and poisoned, and its buildings detroyed, so that no relic might remain of its former existence. Why was this cruel atrocity, as cynically decided upon by the Nazis as was the extermination of the Jews, carried out? Why should the innocent citizens of this village be made the scapegoats for the assassination of Heydrich, who richly deserved his fate? John Bradley was a boy when Lidice was destroyed. An émigré from Moravia, Dr Bradley, now a Senior Lecturer in Government at the University of Manchester, knew the cruelties of both the Nazi and Soviet brands of terror. Dr Bradley explains why Lidice was wiped out, the intricacies of the plot which murdered Heydrich, and the steps which led to this needless tragedy. Through his moving account we can understand why the name of Lidice should and can never be forgotten. In this, the thirtieth anniversary of the holocaust, the victims will bear silent witness to the horrors of war and serve as a reminder, if one were needed, that such an event is an insult to the dignity of mankind and that a repetition of this pointless slaughter of innocent people must never happen again.

The fall of Czechoslovakia

For Czechoslovakia the Second World War started on the fateful 30th day of September 1938 in Munich, when Chamberlain and Daladier, Prime Ministers of Britain and France, together with Mussolini, forced the Czechs to surrender to Chancellor Hitler and the Germans. To the Western powers this regional adjustment, which detached the German frontier areas from Czechoslovakia and which was worked out finally in Munich, without the Czechs even being present, seemed the only solution to the German-Czech problem. Otherwise it was war and no one wanted that.

Events in Czechoslovakia then proceeded at breakneck speed. On 5th October President Beneš resigned and left the country to take up residence in London and prepare a course of lectures in political science for the University of Chicago. A government of national defence, led by the one-eyed hero of the anti-Bolshevik struggle in Siberia in 1918-1920, came to power, but instead of national defence, accepted the terms of the Munich *Diktat* and withdrew its armies from the fortified border areas, letting in the Wehrmacht, without a shot being fired in anger. By abandoning their natural as well as their fortified frontiers, the Czechs were entirely at the mercy of the Germans. Whether

Chamberlain, Daladier, Hitler, Mussolini and Ciano after the agreement at Munich that Germany should 'protect' Czechoslovakia

October 1938. German troops enter Czech territory

German Nazis pull down the border posts along the German-Czechoslovak frontier

the Czechs believed in the Western guarantees of territorial integrity for the truncated Czechoslovakia is open to speculation. When the bitter end came on 15th March 1939 and the Wehrmacht occupied the rest of the Czech territories, no one stirred to enforce the guarantees, or help with the defence. This seems to indicate that the Czechs were resigned to the worst in 1938, and it was the delay which surprised them most.

President Beneš and his successor, President Hácha, had only one hope left for their country: it would regain its sovereignty and independence only after a general European or world conflagration. But this seemed a faint hope, and even as German tanks rolled into Prague and Chancellor Hitler slept in triumph in the castle of the kings of Bohemia, any such prospect appeared far-fetched and very much for the future. Then to every Czech's surprise war came earlier and more unexpectedly than they had dared to hope. After an agreement with Soviet Russia, Hitler invaded Poland and thus sparked off the conflict for which the forlorn Czechs had been waiting so desperately.

Two shadowy figures who would later play leading parts in the story of Lidice, an unknown village near Prague, each made their inauspicious entry in the war. SS-*Obergruppenführer* and General of the Police, Reinhard Heydrich, had made a behind-the-scenes, but nonetheless important, contribution to the outbreak of the war. As the head of the Reich Security Office, he had organised a security takeover in Austria, in the Czech provinces (Bohemia and Moravia) and even in Slovakia which placed itself under the protection of

German armour parades in triumph through Prague's Wenceslas Square after the occupation of the city

4th October 1938. Hitler drives through the Sudetenland, which fell under the 'protection' of the Third Reich

zur POST

Hitler on 14th March 1939. Now in August 1939 Heydrich staged the Gleiwitz incident which became the *casus belli:* his security detachment, disguised in Polish uniforms, attacked the radio station at Gleiwitz and were beaten off by the Gestapo guard. Germany claimed that Poland had attacked her and declared war. It seems strange that with the war keeping him busy all over Europe, Heydrich should have the ambition to rule the Czechs. But busy as he was elsewhere, he gratified this ambition and on 28th September 1941 he arrived in Prague to take charge of these restless provinces of the Reich and cow them into complete submission. It was this appointment that brought about Heydrich's death and the consequent destruction of Lidice.

Lieutenant-Colonel, and later Major-General, František Moravec was one of the Czech Intelligence officers who slipped out of the country on 14th March 1939, just before the Wehrmacht had occupied it. All together eleven officers left by plane and after an adventurous journey, landed at Croydon airport in England. Captain Gibson, the British Military Attaché in Prague, who arranged their departure in a KLM airliner, had done so because the British Intelligence Service was badly in need of these professionals and the Intelligence materials they brought with them. Colonel Moravec, in particular, was useful, for as the head of the large Czech offensive Intelligence, he had agents all over Germany, and above all in the Abwehr, the German counterespionage. Moravec had originally studied classical philology, and in 1915 had gone directly from university to the Eastern Front, been captured by the Russians, joined the Czech Legion in Russia and had thus embarked on his military career. The colonel left his country to avoid the Germans, but he

Acting Reich Protector Heydrich, escorted by Frank, arrives at Prague Castle to take up his new post

had no intention of avoiding the war. From his arrival in Britain he impatiently waited for a chance to serve Czechoslovakia in its struggle against Nazi Germany. But the wait seemed long. At the outbreak of war, in September 1939, Czechoslovakia, which had now shrunk only to the Czech provinces, was *de facto* on the side of Germany. At home, the government in power, however unwillingly, had to collaborate with the occupation authorities, and refused to lead and organise an overt political and military resistance to them. Such a struggle would have to be conducted abroad, mainly in France and Great Britain, (though also in the USSR) where Czechoslovak emigrés were gathered in significant numbers, but for the moment utterly disunited.

The most prestigious Czech living in exile was the former President of Czechoslovakia, Dr Eduard Beneš. He left Czechoslovakia for London where he intended to live and write his memoirs. Just before the occupation of Czechoslovakia by the Wehrmacht, Dr Beneš left Britain for America to deliver a course of lectures at the University of Chicago. When the news of the German occupation of his country broke he protested publicly in his lectures and privately by telegram to President Roosevelt, the French and British Premiers and the Soviet Foreign Minister. But his protests failed to attract Allied attention and only Roosevelt replied (in a routine way) to the telegram. Czechoslovakia seemed forgotten and Dr Beneš with it. However, he was not discouraged; after all he had lived through the long years of the First World War and the Allied neglect of the Czechoslovak cause only to see victory in the end. Now, knowing that war must soon break out, he left Chicago and returned to London to assume the leadership of the Czechoslovak anti-German movement abroad.

On the declaration of war Dr Beneš addressed himself to all the emigré

Czech and Slovak groups in Allied countries, urged them to fight Germany and offered himself as their leader. Reaction to his appeal was divided. In France the Czechs concluded an agreement with the French government and refused to recognise Beneš as their leader. But in Britain the Czech and Slovak residents almost unanimously recognised him. In October 1939 Beneš announced the establishment of the Czechoslovak National Committee which ultimately became the most important political organ of Czech resistance against Germany. But the struggle for recognition, even by the Allies, for whom the Czechs and Slovaks were willing to fight, only just started and was to prove slow and difficult. At first only a few old political friends and allies responded to Beneš's appeal and joined his committee. Colonel

Ex-President of Czechoslovakia Dr Beneš leaves Britain with his wife for a course of lectures in the United States

(future General and President of Czechoslovakia) Svoboda's unit organised in Poland, and then USSR, heard of Beneš's appeal only much later, and was therefore unable to respond at all. But, fortunately for Dr Beneš, the antagonistic French emigré group collapsed and disappeared after the fall of France in 1940. Czechoslovak politicians escaping from France were absorbed into the London Committee and Beneš, its President, decided that the time was propitious to establish a government in exile and ask for international (which at this juncture meant British) recognition.

On 8th July 1940 Dr Beneš sent a letter to Lord Halifax, then Foreign Secretary, in which he informed him that 'the Czechoslovak National Committee in agreement with its army and all the political leaders abroad,

Jan Masaryk. Son of the first President, he was appointed Foreign Minister by the government in exile

but above all in agreement with the unbroken spirit of resistance of the great majority of the population in the occupied motherland (Czechoslovakia) had decided to establish a Provisional Czechoslovak government with the necessary administration as far as possible in Great Britain.' A fortnight later, Lord Halifax replied that the British government recognised this Provisional Czechoslovak government as an Allied government and henceforth began to treat it as a government in exile, assuming, among other things, financial responsibility for it.

This was a tremendous victory for Beneš and the Czechoslovak emigré cause; from then on Beneš began to consider himself as the reinstated constitutional President of Czechoslovakia. He also believed that British recognition of himself and his government meant a tacit repudiation of the Munich agreement. By fighting in the war, the Czechoslovaks would gradually bring about public and explicit repudiations of the Munich *Diktat*, and after the war the Allies, who in 1938–9 agreed to dismember his country, would recreate it. Such were his hopes.

Meanwhile, however, he appointed a government which was to organise the struggle against Germany. He had enough politicians at hand to appoint even a sort of parliament, the State Council, which in the unreal world of exile gave a certain constitutional weight to the President and his government. Šrámek, aged and venerable member of many prewar coalition cabinets, became Prime Minister, and Jan Masaryk, son of the first President of Czechoslovakia, became Foreign Minister. However, the most important job in the government, that of Minister of War, went to General Ingr, a tough professional soldier, who immediately set up a war office and general staff. He had in Britain a small air force, numerous infantry units and a small but efficient nucleus of Intelligence

Monseigneur Jan Šrámek, wartime
President of Czechoslovakia

General Ingr, Minister of War
in Beneš's government

service. On 24th July 1940 a jubilant President Beneš told the Czechoslovak people over the BBC that their nation existed once again, internationally recognised by the Allies. After the war he would come back home to take over where he had left off in 1938.

It was obvious to every Czechoslovak abroad that this kind of jubilation was premature. A lot of fighting and sacrifice lay ahead before Dr Beneš' dream would come true, but the practical Czechs began their fight immediately. Their pilots, after an escape from France, were already fighting in several squadrons (310, 312 and later on 313) of the RAF Fighter Command. The RAF Bomber Command had at its disposal the entirely Czech 311 Squadron. In addition many Czechs and Slovaks were fighting in the 1st and 68th Night Fighter Squadrons as well as in the 9th, 11th and 601st Fighter Squadrons. One of the most successful Czech fighter pilots, J František DFC, ironically served in the Polish 303rd Fighter Squadron. Although two Czechoslovak infantry divisions were formed in France, they were completely destroyed and demoralised by the collapse of France. Many Czech soldiers managed to escape to Britain, but the British could only field a Czechoslovak brigade with some 3,276 men, and more than a fifth (700) of the men serving in this unit were officers. The Czechs and Slovaks did relatively little actual fighting, but from 1941 concentrated on intensive Intelligence activity. With the establishment of SOE, many professional Czech and Slovak soldiers were detailed to special duties and operations in this organisation. The aim of SOE was to involve the Czechs and Slovaks in actual fighting on their own soil, both as Intelligence agents and resistance fighters. This peculiar mixture of Intelligence and underground activity suited the Czech special agents very well. Czechoslovak Intelligence officers, who had sought refuge in Britain in 1939, were in charge of these operations from the

21

Czech troops newly arrived from France march into their camp in England

beginning, and gave them an unmistakable character and as Intelligence operations these SOE missions proved extremely successful. Thus in 1940 a tremendous success was scored when Czech agents managed to obtain, and radio out of the Reich, Hitler's plan, 'Sea Lion', for the invasion of Great Britain.

The Czechoslovak political leadership in Britain had maintained political contacts with Czechoslovakia through couriers at first, then in 1940, Dr Krajina, a resistance leader, succeeded in establishing direct radio contact with London (Sparta I). He maintained this contact until May 1941 when the Gestapo discovered and destroyed his transmitter. Though a military resistance group had another transmitter (Sparta II) this was also located by the Gestapo

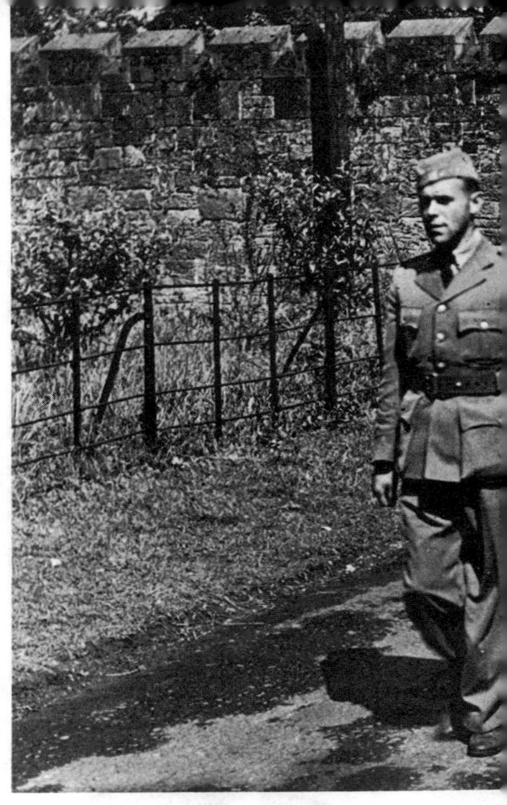

Czech pilots serving with the Royal Air Force

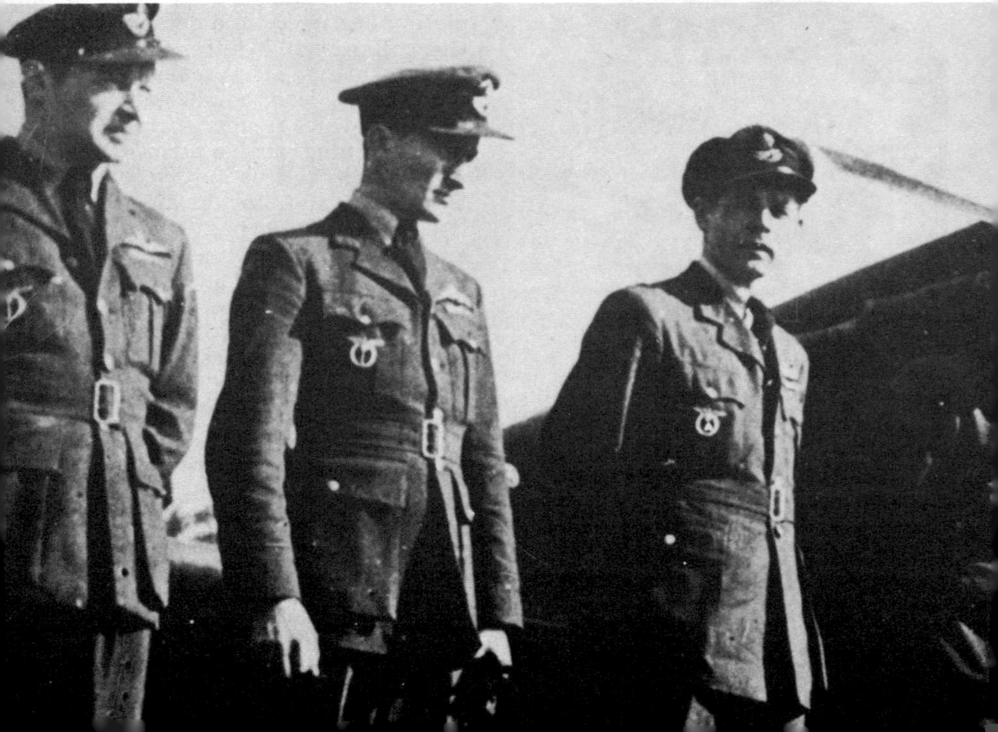

The dismembering of Czechoslovakia 1938-1944
Boundary of Czechoslovakia Sept. 1938
International boundaries Sept. 1938
Territory occupied by Germany, 5th Oct. 1938
Territory ceded to Hungary, dates as shown
0 Miles 120
0 Kilometres 200
Warsaw
GERMANY
Elbe
Oder
Leipzig
Thuringia
Dresden
SILESIA
Breslau
Gleiwitz
POLAND
Cracow
Vistula
Lwow
SUDETENLAND
Terezin
Lidice
Prague
Labe
Pardubice
Ležáky
M. Ostrava
BOHEMIA
(German Protectorate: 15th Mar. 1939)
Pilsen
Vltava
Bernartice
Kroměříz
MORAVIA
(German Prot. 15th Mar. 1939)
Brno
SLOVAKIA
(German Protectorate: 14th Mar. 1939)
Klak
Kosice
RUTHENIA
(to Hungary 14th Mar. 1939)
Mauthausen
Danube
Munich
Bratislava
(to Hungary 2nd Oct. 1938)
Vienna
AUSTRIA
Budapest
HUNGARY
RUMANIA

Staff Sergeant J Valčík of Silver A Commando

Staff Sergeant Josef Gabčík of Anthropoid Commando

who surprised the operators while in the process of transmitting a message. Colonel Mašín, seriously wounded, was captured by the Gestapo, but although his two fellow officers shot their way out of the ambush, the transmitter was lost.

To maintain and strengthen these vital contacts, both for Intelligence and political reasons, the British and the Czechoslovaks decided to stiffen the resistance movement with special agents. This operation proved immensely difficult. The first fully trained Czech parachutist, special agent O Riedl, was dropped in Central Europe in April 1941: but instead of landing in central Bohemia he landed near Landeck in the Tyrolian Alps, and was arrested. However, he succeeded in convincing the authorities that he was an innocent Czech making his way to Switzerland, and after a short prison sentence he was deported back to his native Moravia and survived the war to tell the tale.

Despite this failure, both the British and emigré Czechs forged on in their efforts. The former desperately needed Intelligence from the Reich and the latter wanted to alleviate the plight of the Czech resistance movement.

Between May 1941 and April 1942 some twenty-seven parachutists, specially trained for their tasks, were dropped in Czechoslovakia to strengthen and reorganise the underground network. But it proved a terrible uphill struggle: transmitters failed to arrive, or when they did, failed to work. Thus London was forced to send more and more men and equipment to Czechoslovakia. In December 1941 three more missions were dispatched. They were the most important groups ever dropped in the occupied country: 'Silver A' commando consisting of Lieutenant A Bartoš, Staff Sergeant J Valčík and radio operator J Potůček. Their task was to re-establish contact with the resistance and keep liaison with London. 'Silver B' commando actually transported the radio transmitter and were to be responsible for its operations. To 'Anthropoid' commando, consisting of Staff Sergeants Jan Kubiš and Jozef Gabčík, was given the most secret and important task: the assassination of SS-*Obergruppenführer und General der Polizei* Reinhard Heydrich, who, in September 1941, was appointed as Acting Protector of Bohemia and Moravia.

Resistance and assassination

The Czechs and Slovaks never gave up the hope of re-establishing their state. The 'puppet' governments of Czechoslovakia from 1938 to 1939 led Czech opposition to the Germans and was the centre of Czech resistance against German encroachments. For international reasons Hitler declared the Czech provinces autonomous, and not annexed territories, within the German Reich. From the very beginning of the occupation, on 15th March 1939, he was obliged to listen to all sorts of advice on the solution of the Czech problem, and in September 1939, he made his decision. As long as the war lasted the Czechs were to be exploited economically, ruthlessly and by all means available, but the 'final solution' would be made after the war. But this decision did not mean that the Czechs would be left in peace to work for the German war machine. Hitler appointed as State Secretary (later German minister) for the Protectorate, the Sudeten German leader, Karl Hermann Frank: he was responsible for the execution of all policies initiated by either the Protector, or Bormann or even Hitler himself relating to the Czech problem. Frank was a chauvinist who wanted to Germanise the Czechs and kill off those who did not want to be or could not be Germanised. (Cf his memorandum of 29th September 1940.) In such a position of power, Frank was able to carry out his own policy unhindered, even despite Hitler's decisions. Though he was

Symbol of German occupation for the people of Czechoslovakia

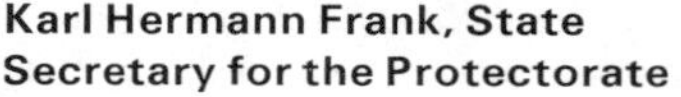

**Karl Hermann Frank, State
Secretary for the Protectorate**

always careful to cover himself and find suitable pretexts for his 'final solutions', he quickly became the chief executioner of the Czechs. It was, above all, against him and other extremists of his kind that the Czech government took up the cause of resistance.

After the occupation of the Czech provinces, in March 1939, General Blaskowitz eclipsed for a time the Czech President, Dr Hácha, and his government: for over a month the German Wehrmacht ruled the country directly. But on 7th April 1939 Hitler appointed as Protector and his chief representative in the Czech provinces, the German diplomat, Freiherr von Neurath. This appointment seemed a conciliatory move but was soon counterbalanced by Frank's arrival. A fortnight after Neurath's appearance in Prague, a new Czech government was appointed by President Hácha. General Eliáš, the new Premier, was a professional soldier and the majority of his cabinet, including himself, were members of the masonic order (a crime in the eyes of Hitler and the Nazis) and were all friends of the former President, Beneš, with whom they maintained contact. This was not a collaborationist government: in time it would even assume the leadership of resistance to the Germans, for the Czechs were convinced that a time for resistance would soon come. Some time before this 'government of resistance' was appointed the Czechs began to organise their anti-German movement. On the very day of the occupation the Czech communists formed their underground central

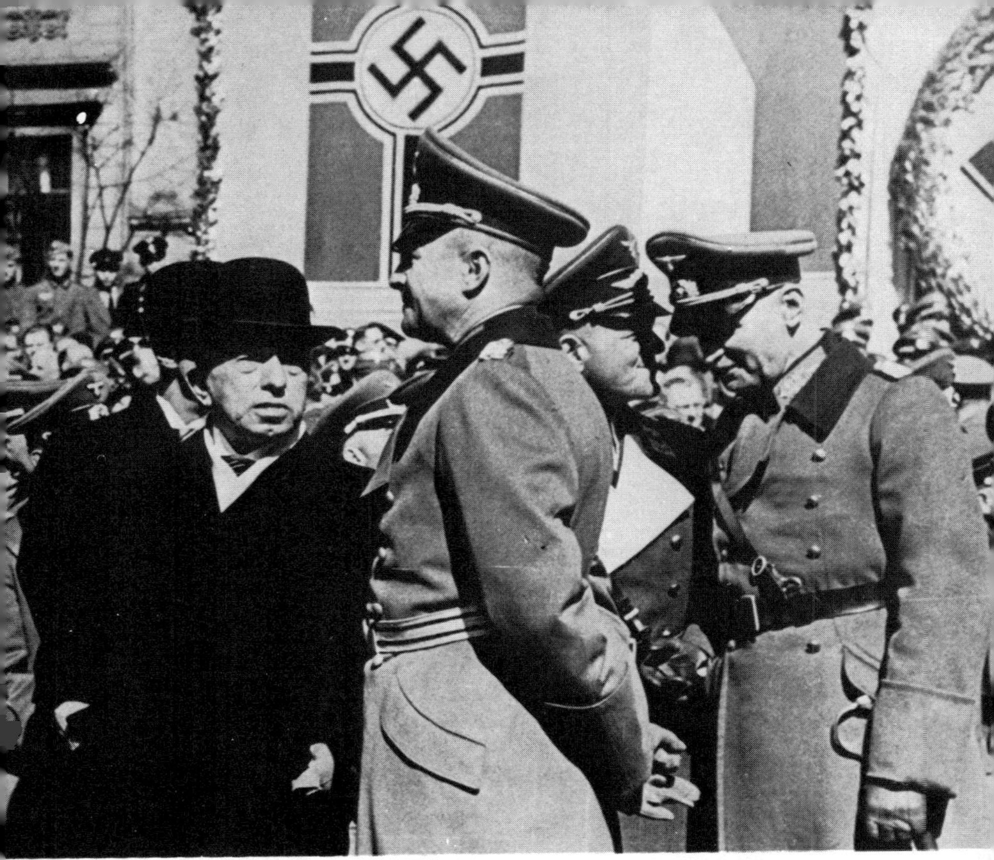

committee and the pro-Beneš ele-
ments organised the Political Centre
(*politické ústředí*) which perhaps a
little paradoxically was more an
Intelligence agency than a political
movement. Shortly afterwards many
intellectuals and professional soldiers
formed the National Defence Organisation (*Obrana národa*) which was a
political movement with an Intelligence section. This not only maintained contacts with Dr Beneš in
London, but also co-ordinated
national resistance at home and co-
operated with the communists. Premier Eliáš was deeply involved in
both organisations.

At the time of the German occupation the Czechs were not particularly
well prepared for resistance. They
had only limited experience in this
type of warfare dating back to the
First World War and their ideas

**Freiherr von Neurath with President
Hácha and Generals Brauchitsch,
Milch and Blaskowitz**

were rather unreal. But soon German
persecutions drove home the realisa-
tion that resistance would have to be
organised if the very existence of the
Czech nation was not to be put in
jeopardy. On the official level, both
President Hácha and Premier
Eliáš's government tried their best
to protect the Czechs: on the un-
official level the existing resistance
organisations also began to do their
best and seek out allies against the
Germans. Obviously these allies had
to be found among Germany's opponents and soon Intelligence contacts were established with the French
and the British. In 1939 this seemed
the best defensive/offensive move: the
Obrana národa created a large military

Frank inspects an illegal Communist press discovered by the Gestapo in Prague

The State Secretary inspects confiscated insignia from the disbanded Charles University in Prague

branch to satisfy the Western Allies; and it was rightly assumed that political alliances would be sought and concluded by Dr Beneš. The brunt of German persecutions fell at first on the outlawed Czech communist party and in the first two months of the German occupation the majority of some 4,639 Czechs arrested by the Gestapo were communists. When war broke out and the Gestapo got wind of Czech Intelligence contacts, some 9,300 people were arrested, mainly army officers, intellectuals and students who were suspected of contacts with the Western Powers. However, the first wave of bloody persecutions was in a sense forced on the Germans: the Czech political underground movement got over its paralysis after the outbreak of the war and began to show signs of life.

It is paradoxical that while the Czechs were armed but alone against the Germans they did nothing; when disarmed and defenceless, but with allies, they showed defiance and bravery which bordered on mass death-wish. By October 1939 Poland was destroyed and the whole of Europe lived in terror and anticipation of the next German strike, but the Czech underground movement was now busy organising anti-German demonstrations to commemorate the anniversary of the foundation of their independent state which no longer existed. Out of the blue, on 28th October 1939, the first organised demonstrations and strikes took place all over the country and in Prague Frank made good use of them. He ordered the German police to disperse the Czechs by force of arms and many were killed and wounded. On 15th November 1939 demonstrations recurred during the funeral of one of the victims, a student of Prague University J Opletal. They were again ruthlessly repressed. Two days later the Staatssekretär K H Frank struck hard against the Czechs: all universities were closed down for three years, a large number of students and intellectuals were arrested and sent to concentration camps, nine youth leaders were shot outright. Martial law was proclaimed in Prague and the surrounding districts and President Hácha was forced to broadcast an appeal to the Czechs to remain calm and orderly. The real struggle had now begun and the brutal execution of nine innocent Czech youth leaders not involved in the demonstrations, made clear to everybody what the struggle was about. The Czechs reacted vigorously to the rule of K H Frank. As German pressure was intensified Intelligence activity increased and direct help from Britain was accepted. Contacts with the Czechoslovak resistance abroad were established; the emigré movement was swollen by Czech and Slovak officers and men who escaped to the West to continue their fight against the national enemy; signifiant numbers of prominent Czech politicians began to leave the protectorate, joining the political movement of resistance abroad led by Dr Beneš and courier contacts were supplemented by underground radio links with London.

Needless to say this increased activity did not go unobserved by Frank who, in addition to the Gestapo (some 2,000 men), had several other security and police organisations at his disposal (*Sicherheitspolizei* – some 600 men, *Kriminalpolizei*, *Sicherheitsdienst* SD – some 1,600 men). These security organisations had branches and networks all over the country and in the main cities of Bohemia and Moravia and proved efficient for dealing with the Czech resistance movement and SOE agents coming from Britain. In fact throughout the war the Czech provinces were extremely well guarded and policed. The bulk of the repressive forces was formed by the 539 and 540 Wehrmacht armies. Three divisions (Grenzwache division, the 193rd and 154th) were quartered in all the larger towns and were supplemented by a large network of training and anti-aircraft units. In addition, many SS formations had their home bases in the Czech provinces. Overall numbers differed from year to year (6-15 divisions) but the most conservative estimate of all army and security forces was 200,000 men. The administration was also thoroughly 'Germanised' and there was one German official to 790 Czechs (comparative figures were 3,608 for Norway, 5,512 for Holland, 5,872 for France, 9,348 for Belgium, 42,696 for Denmark, etc).

Late in 1939 and early in 1940 the *Obrana národa* was decimated by the Gestapo. The Political Centre, some of whose members were in the Czech

The changing of the guard at the King's Castle in Prague, the residence of Reich Protector Heydrich

government, came next. Many leaders (and two ministers) saw the danger and escaped from the country to Britain to join Dr Beneš. Many others were arrested, tried and some were executed: the last included ultimately the brave Premier, General Eliáš, and many immediate family members of politicians who had fled the country. Only the left-wing group *Věrni zůstaneme* somehow survived this wave of repression. But the military-intelligence group of the *Obrana národa* led by Generals Bílý and Homola was able to continue its work and maintain its contacts with Colonel Moravec, the Czech Intelligence chief in London.

However, in 1940 the resistance movement was seriously disorganised by wholesale arrests and executions. Nevertheless, despite tremendous losses, new enthusiasts were joining the movement and risking their lives to do its work. It was at this stage that the London Czechs decided to stiffen the largely amateurish groups at home with specially trained professional agents from Britain, and as soon as weather permitted they began to drop them into Czechslovakia itself. These professionals would reorganise and unite the movement and prepare it for significant operations against the Germans.

In 1941 the Czech communists finally agreed to join the National Central Revolutionary Committee and the resistance had a united political centre. So far, however, very little resisting was actually done: the work consisted almost entirely of collecting and transmitting Intelligence material to London. This was now going to be intensified and other operations, such as sabotage, were being planned. In June 1940, on instructions from

April 1942. Heydrich inspects officers
of the Security Service School, Prague

Colonel Moravec, Captain Morávek, of *Obrana národa*, re-established contact with a German double agent and head of the Abwehr organisation in Prague, Paul Thümmel, who had been an important source of Intelligence in the past. Now Thümmel began to hand over plans against the USSR, and also helped with timely warnings against Gestapo arrests. He even procured spare parts for radio transmitters, when the Czechs were in need of them. On 27th March 1941 Captain Morávek reported to London that Thümmel had told him: 'The campaign against the USSR was definitely decided upon. As soon as the campaign in Jugoslavia is completed, Germany will advance against the USSR. . . the date for the state of war preparedness (*Kriegsbereitschaft*) for the Eastern front is 15th May 1941'. On 3rd April 1941 the British Premier, Winston Churchill, passed on this message to Joseph Stalin who decided not to believe it.

In the summer of 1941 the Gestapo finally traced two resistance transmitters, Sparta I and II, despite Thümmel's warning, cornered and caught several resistance leaders and radio operators. After this success with the transmitters, it became obvious to the Germans that the resistance network had recovered from the shocks of 1940. On 10th June 1941 *Staatssekretär* Frank reported to

Hitler: 'By discovering the Intelligence transmitters we have scored an immense success; we also uncovered a non-communist network which nonetheless worked for the USSR . . . thanks to this Gestapo blow we can consider this particular Czech underground movement as liquidated'. But he added ominously: 'However, the place of the liquidated group was taken up by another, albeit numerically weaker, but even more dangerous group which concentrates on Intelligence and sabotage work.' But luck was on the German side, and between July and October 1941, this dangerous group, *Věrni zůstaneme*, consisting mainly of trade union leaders, was betrayed and gradually arrested and liquidated.

However, by then the Gestapo had even more dangerous resistance opponents to face: the parachutists from Britain.

Paradoxically, the parachute operations were started from the USSR. On 10th September 1941 four Czech soldiers were dropped from a Soviet aircraft near Kroměříž and three were captured almost immediately. One of them, J Kasík, not only betrayed his friends and fellow soldiers, but also changed sides and became a Gestapo agent. As a result of this 'successful' drop 160 Czechs who had co-operated with the commando were arrested and sent to Nazi concentration camps. The Gestapo tried to use Kasík for the *Funkspiel* with the USSR, but Thümmel told Captain Morávek about his betrayal and Moscow was warned via London. It was at this point that Colonel Moravec decided to send one of his best trained men to Czechoslovakia. F Pavelka, twenty-one year-old officer-cadet, was specially recommended for the operation by his commanding officer, Major Edwards. His mission, codenamed 'Percentage', was to re-establish the badly mauled contacts with Czechoslovakia. He was to be dropped in Czechoslovakia between 3rd and 7th October. Since he was bringing a new transmitter and explosives Pavelka was awaited with great impatience. However, the welcoming party missed him as he was dropped too far west; Pavelka nonetheless made his contacts with the underground, had the transmitter and explosives ready for delivery, but on 25th October was suddenly arrested while hiding in Prague. It was later learned that he had been betrayed by the arrested members of the underground group, for whom he brought the transmitter, codes and explosives. After a long interrogation Pavelka was executed in January 1943. He did not betray anything that the Gestapo did not know already; however, as early as this first case, the name of Lidice came up – Pavelka had two addresses of Lidice people who would help him in case of trouble. After

Heydrich's assassination these addresses, now carefully filed, would prove fatal to the entire village.

In December 1941, after several postponements, three important missions were dropped in Czechoslovakia, (codenamed 'Silver A' and 'B' and 'Anthropoid'). While the 'Silver' missions were to renew liaison between London and the Czech resistance, 'Anthropoid's' task was to assassinate the new Protector, Heydrich. 'Silver A' and 'B' commandoes had to cope with great difficulties on landing and making contact. But their commander, Lieutenant Bartoš proved a resourceful man and soon made contacts with the resistance movement, especially with the military group of the *Obrana národa*. He eventually reached Captain Morávek and could transmit his messages to London: Thümmel was again supplying the Czechs with Intelligence material. However, tragedy struck only a week after this success. On 21st March 1942 Captain Morávek arrived unexpectedly at a meeting in a Prague park which was betrayed to the Gestapo. The park was surrounded and when Captain Moravek tried to shoot his way out, as he had done many times before, he was seriously wounded and rather than fall alive into the Gestapo's hands he shot himself. On his dead body the Gestapo found important coded signals from London and the photograph of Valčík, one of the 'Silver A' parachutists, who had to instantly go into hiding, for the Gestapo traced him to his cover address at Pardubice. Meanwhile, further missions arrived from Britain: 'Zinc', 'Out Distance', 'Bivouac', 'Bioscope', 'Intransitive', 'Tin', 'Antimony', 'Bronze' and 'Iridium'. New resistance groups were organised, or put in touch with the London centre, and it seemed that the resistance movement despite its setbacks, was flourishing and possibly even getting beyond the control of the German occupation forces.

The Protector of Czechoslovakia, Freiherr von Neurath, became 'ill' at about this time and Hitler replaced him by a tough man of his own choice. The chauvinist Sudeten German, Frank, was passed over and in September 1941 Hitler's security expert and head of the *Reichssicherheitsamt*, Reinhard Heydrich, moved to Prague as Acting Protector. On his arrival he immediately demonstrated what he meant by protection: 'For the protection of German interests I hereby proclaim martial law in the territories of Bohemia and Moravia which takes effect from 28th September 1941. All acts against public order, economic life as well as labour peace together with the unlawful possession of firearms, explosives or ammunition, will be judged under this law. All assemblies in private rooms or public highways are forbidden. There will be no appeal against the sentences of these court martials. Sentences will be carried out immediately by shooting or hanging. Signed: Heydrich.' This was Heydrich's 'policy of pacification' of the Czechs (*Peitsche und Zucker*). In concrete terms this meant that 142 Czechs were executed and 584 sent to concentration camps on the very day of the Protector's arrival. In October 1941 the terror increased still further: 248 Czechs were sentenced to death and executed, while 953 were shipped to the death camp at Mauthausen. However, Heydrich had even more far reaching plans for the destruction of Czech political and social life.

On 11th November 1941, Prime Minister General Eliáš was unceremoniously arrested and Heydrich started to put in motion his schemes for the 'final solution' of the Czech problem. This time *Staatssekretär* Frank had found sympathetic ears for his ideas: some Czechs would be 'Germanised' and the rest resettled possibly in the arctic north of Soviet Russia. Hey-

Reinhard Heydrich, security expert, head of the *Reichssicherheitsamt* and target for assassination

drich's most immediate plan was to reduce the Czech provinces to the status of Saxony or Bavaria within the Third Reich. On 6th November 1941 Heydrich wrote to Bormann, Hitler's *éminence grise*, that he would destroy Czech autonomy by private instructions. His first move in this respect followed in January 1942 when he dissolved the cabinet government, already headless, and appointed individual ministers whose freedom of action was further hampered by German officials acting as secretaries of state.

On 23rd January, Heydrich again wrote to Bormann and told him that through his reform, the Czech government ceased to be a centre for collecting complaints against the Reich. It must now become an active tool of the Protector against the Czech population itself. Since the Czechs also had to be exploited economically as much as was feasible, the policy of terror was supplemented by special acts of favour: additional food rations went to workers who increased productivity, especially in war industries. As in the Reich, peaceful and hard-working Czech workers were sent for holidays to spas, which they could not have afforded before the war. Cigarettes were also distributed as special production bonuses. Heydrich really believed that his combination of 'whip and sugar' (*Peitsche und Zucker*) would work with the Czechs. Only ten days before his assassination, Heydrich reported to Bormann that the memories of the terror unleashed on his arrival in 1941, had begun to wane and suggested that new waves of repression should be prepared so that he could continue to run the Czech provinces successfully.

But unknowingly on his arrival in Prague Heydrich had signed his own death warrant by ordering the 'preventive' executions of General Bílý and Vojta: apart from being members

Heydrich in Prague on the day he assumed power, with Frank

of the resistance movement, the two generals were friends of the chief Intelligence officer in London, Colonel Moravec. He had already despatched his avengers to Prague.

Shortly after the fall of France in 1940, SOE and the Czechoslovak Intelligence Department began to pick and train special agents. It is not quite clear how closely these two services co-operated, but it seems that the Czechs, for. services rendered previously, were particularly favoured and enjoyed considerable independence. It was mainly the professional Intelligence officers, above all Colonel Moravec, the chief, who were responsible for handpicking the men. However, once selected, the Czechs went through the usual SOE training. First of all they passed through commando training at Mallaigh in Scotland: Major Young took them through the usual SOE Special Training School which included map reading and 'silent' killing. Next they were transferred to Manchester Airport, where Major Edwards and his staff taught them how to jump out of an aircraft safely. The training was then completed in Surrey at Castle Bellasis near Dorking where they learned how to code radio messages, handle arms and explosives and shoot accurately and instinctively in any situation. However, the final political training and Intelligence briefing was left to the Czechs: the Czech Intelligence HQ was in London, at 134 Piccadilly. Czech officers had to judge whether the men could be sent back to Czechoslovakia, to carry out political and Intelligence missions and face death, for in case of failure there was no return to base. In September 1941 Colonel Moravec had at his disposal quite a number of these special agents to retaliate against the executioner of the Czechs.

To trace the origin of the decision

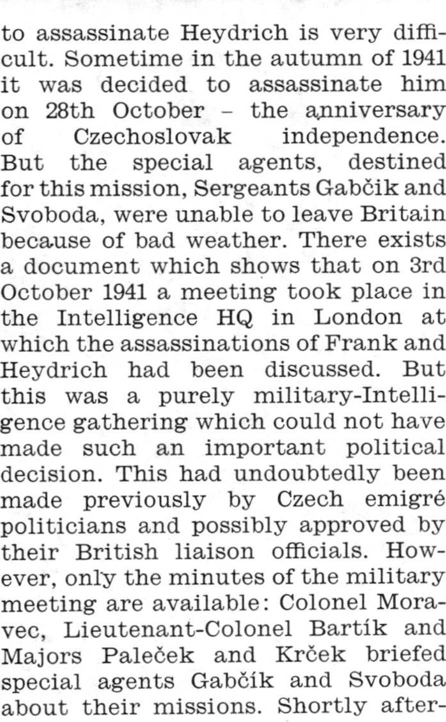

Lieutenant-Colonel (here as Colonel) Bartík briefed Anthropoid Commando on its mission

to assassinate Heydrich is very difficult. Sometime in the autumn of 1941 it was decided to assassinate him on 28th October – the anniversary of Czechoslovak independence. But the special agents, destined for this mission, Sergeants Gabčik and Svoboda, were unable to leave Britain because of bad weather. There exists a document which shows that on 3rd October 1941 a meeting took place in the Intelligence HQ in London at which the assassinations of Frank and Heydrich had been discussed. But this was a purely military-Intelligence gathering which could not have made such an important political decision. This had undoubtedly been made previously by Czech emigré politicians and possibly approved by their British liaison officials. However, only the minutes of the military meeting are available: Colonel Moravec, Lieutenant-Colonel Bartík and Majors Paleček and Krček briefed special agents Gabčik and Svoboda about their missions. Shortly after-

wards Svoboda injured himself and bad weather put a stop to this urgent mission. Kubiš was then selected to replace Svoboda and a new commando, codenamed 'Anthropoid', was ready to be dropped in Czechoslovakia. Only shortly before leaving the two NCOs were finally instructed to kill Heydrich and not Frank.

On 28th December 1941 at 10pm 'Anthropoid' together with 'Silver A' and 'B' left Tangmere airport aboard a Halifax aircraft. The Canadian crew was to drop them in three pre-arranged locations inside Czechoslovakia, but none of the missions landed in the locality where they were expected. 'Anthropoid' came down ten miles north of Prague, instead of in western Bohemia, near Pilsen. With their boxes of explosives and firearms the landing itself was extremely dangerous, for this was a thickly populated area. Furthermore, on landing Sergeant Gabčik injured his foot which caused him a lot of pain. They hid their parachutes, left their air

Stormtroopers guard the magnificent
Mathias Gate of the King's Castle

Halifaxes were used to drop SOE operatives in countries occupied by the Germans

overalls and helmets in a hut in the field nearby, and it was not until dawn when they were ready to walk into Pilsen that they discovered that they had landed in the wrong place, and would be forced to fend for themselves, instead of making contact with the underground.

They failed to find woods but came across a quarry, where they decided to set up emergency headquarters. They were soon discovered by local people, and this time their luck held. Some Czechs, good patriots, fed them and then put them in touch with the resistance group 'Jindra', whose field of operations was in Prague. Both parachutists were taken care of, provided with genuine identity cards, ration cards and placed in safe quarters in the city. On 12th January 1942 Kubiš returned to the place of landing and disposed of the two para-

chutes. He then went to Pilsen for a few days in order to follow the planned route and though the people in Pilsen were helpful, Kubiš returned to Prague, where he felt safer. The visit to Pilsen was indispensable, for the two men were thus able to re-establish contact with 'Silver A' and through it with London. Early in March 1942 Lieutenant Bartoš could signal London that he was in touch with Gabčík and Kubiš via Pilsen. They were working on an estate near Prague, but living in the city. London could issue final orders to both men to accomplish their mission.

London headquarters do not seem to have been in a hurry to send the final signal. On 14th April 1942 Kubiš received an order to go to Pilsen again and with the help of another parachutist, Valčík, to start fires in the neighbourhood of the Škoda works to mark them for a bombing raid by the RAF; the works were pouring out German panzers.

Protector Heydrich lived in a vil-

1273

Army Book 64 (Part I).

Soldier's Service Book.

(Soldier's Pay Book, Army Book 64 (Part II), will be issued for active service.)

Entries in this book (other than those connected with the making of a Soldier's Will and insertion of the names of relatives) are to be made under the superintendence of an Officer.

Instructions to Soldier.

1. You are held **personally responsible** for the safe custody of this book.

2. You will **always carry this book** on your person.

3. You must produce the book whenever called upon to do so by a competent military authority, viz., Officer, Warrant Officer, N.C.O. or Military Policeman.

4. You must not alter or make any entry in this book (except as regards your next-of-kin on pages 10 and 11 or your Will on pages 15 to 20).

5. Should you lose the book you will report the matter to your immediate military superior.

6. On your transfer to the Army Reserve this book will be handed into your Orderly Room for transmission, through the O. i/c Records, to place of rejoining on mobilization.

7. You will be permitted to retain this book after discharge, but should you lose the book after discharge it cannot be replaced.

8. If you are discharged from the Army Reserve, this book will be forwarded to you by the O. i/c Records.

The British army Service Book of Jan Kubiš, last minute replacement for the injured Svoboda

lage, Panenské Brežany, just outside Prague. He had taken over a manor house confiscated from a Jewish family; it had a large orchard and wooded park, which he used for horse riding. Every morning a Mercedes car drove up to the house and Heydrich's personal chauffeur drove the acting Protector to Prague. The car drove through the village, climbed a hill, and before reaching the main road to the capital, was joined by an armed escort which usually accompanied it up to the suburbs. Sometimes the Protector's car was escorted to the royal castle, Hradčany, where he had his office.

Kubiš and Gabčík thus began to visit the village and observe cars and drivers. Regularly, they cycled along the roads and tried to pick the most suitable place for the assassination. At first they thought they could capture Heydrich alive, somewhere near Mělník, where he went often without an escort. Their next scheme was to place a bomb in his room or shoot him near Chotek Park in Prague, where he occasionally went. Then they thought the most suitable place would be just outside the village, when the car slowed down to climb the hill. But the armed escort was uncomfortably near and they therefore chose the suburb, Libeň-Holešovičky. On 19th and 20th May Lieutenant Bartoš received two specially coded telegrams for 'Anthropoid'. This was London's final confirmation of orders: the assassination was to be carried out on 27th May. By that time, it was a meticulously planned operation.

On 23rd May Professor Vaněk, a resistance leader, visited Dr K Novotný whose brother, a watchmaker, had repaired watches in the Hradčany office that very day. The watchmaker had found out that Heydrich planned to fly to Hitler on 27th May. 'Anthropoid' was immediately informed and the two NCOs made final preparations with Lieutenant Opálka. After the assassination it was decided to seize Heydrich's briefcase which would undoubtedly be full of important documents. To get the briefcase intact Heydrich was to die by automatic fire: grenades were to be used only in an emergency. Along the route and on the spot, apart from the two agents, underground men were posted to signal and cause diversions if necessary. On 27th May, towards 9 am three cyclists arrived at Libeň at the tram stop, V Holešovičkách. One of them, Valčík of 'Silver B', continued farther up the hill, while the others, Gabčík and Kubiš of 'Anthropoid', came to a halt not far from the stop which was at the end of a sharp bend. They leant their bicycles against the fence; Kubiš stationed himself on the bend and prepared two of his special grenades, which he had brought with him from Britain. Twenty yards farther up the hill, Gabčík unlocked his Sten gun and hid it under his raincoat. Two hundred yards farther still, on top of the hill, was Valčík waiting to give them a signal with his mirror when the car approached. It took the assassins about half an hour to take up their positions trying to look as inconspicuous as was possible. Lieutenant Opálka also arrived to check the men's positions. All three were excited and Opálka tried to calm them. Now everything was ready: the rest depended on Heydrich.

For Reinhard Heydrich 27th May was a special day. He was to drive to his office as usual, but after supervising the day's business he was to board his special Junkers 52 and fly to Berlin to attend to the security problems of the Reich, for he was still in charge of the *Reichsicherheitsamt*. That day his Mercedes would not be driven by his personal chauffeur, but by his bodyguard SS-*Oberscharführer* Klein. The family farewell delayed Heydrich and he did not order his armed escort to accompany him, for it would have delayed him still further. Klein drove as fast as he could towards Prague. The assassins were nervously waiting for the de-

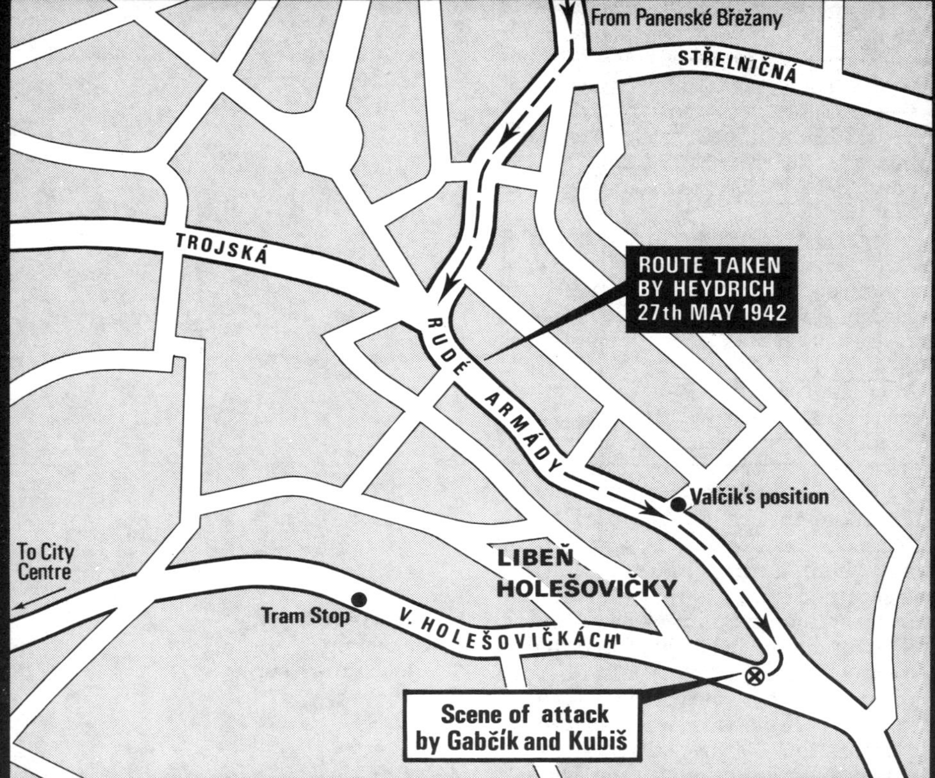

The assassins' attack on Heydrich

layed Protector: Valčík smoked one cigarette after another, when suddenly he caught sight of the fast moving Mercedes. Immediately he took out of his pocket a comb and a small mirror. He combed his hair and, using the mirror, signalled to his friends below that the car was approaching.

Before the Mercedes drew parallel to the waiting men, they received another signal: resistance members passed by in another car telling them that Heydrich was alone without his armed escort. Gabčík and Kubiš were ready; they saw the car approaching them, and as it got within a few yards of Gabčík he jumped from the pavement on to the tram track, pulled out the Stengun from under his coat and tried to open fire at the car. Klein driving the car saw Gabčík pointing his gun at them, but it remained silent: it was jammed. Klein's reaction was to pull out his own gun and have a shot at the assassin, instead of driving as fast as he could out of this obvious ambush. The Mercedes slowed down as it reached Kubiš who was puzzled by his comrade's failure to fire; but he was perfectly calm, pulled out the pin of his grenade and threw it at the car. The heavily damaged car came to a stop, and Klein, who was unharmed, jumped out with his pistol drawn, chasing back to shoot the luckless Gabčík. The latter had seen the explosion and finally realised that his gun was useless. He threw it away and ran down the street towards the city with Klein close behind shooting wildly. The chase went on for some considerable time, but then Gabčík pulled out his other pistol, hit the SS man several times and immobilised him. He then jumped into the first tram going towards the city centre and disappeared from the scene. Kubiš, who had thrown the bomb from too short a distance, was injured by the blast and his face was bleeding heavily. Nevertheless, he ran across the road to his bicycle, followed by the injured Protector, who was too shock-

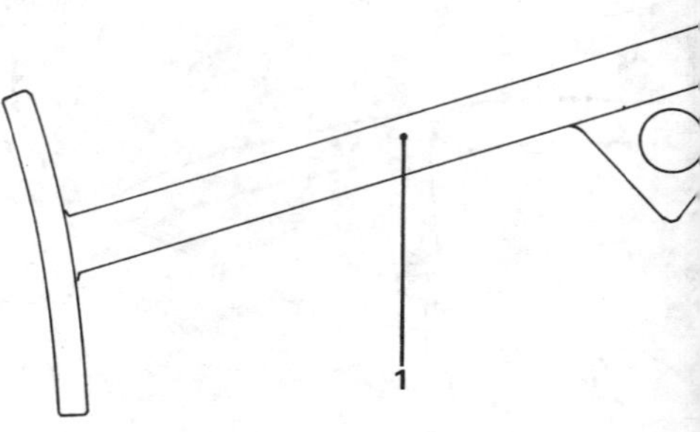

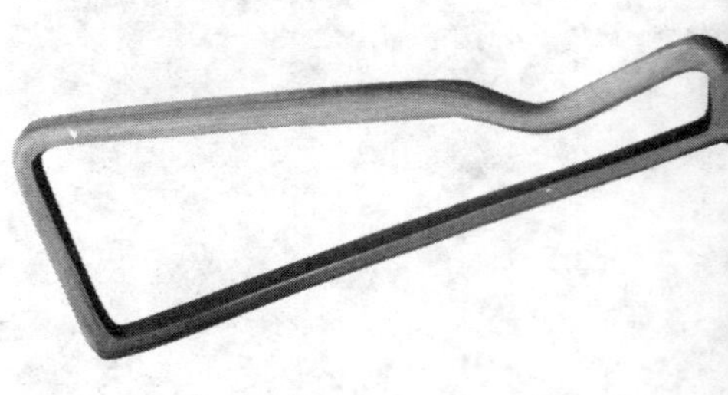

1 Steel tube butt
2 Backsight
3 Block return spring
4 Trigger pin
5 Trigger

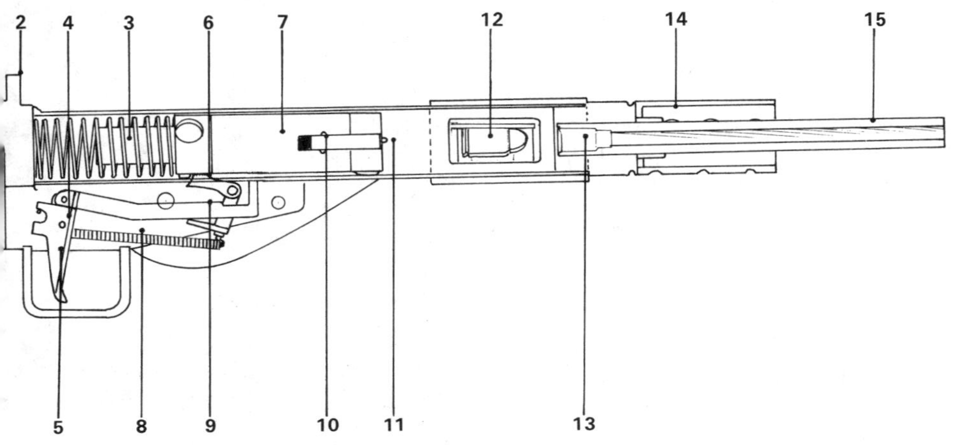

6	Sear	11	Firing pin
7	Breech block assembly	12	32 9mm rounds
8	Trigger return spring	13	Chamber
9	Trip lever	14	Barrel sleeve
10	Extractor	15	Barrel

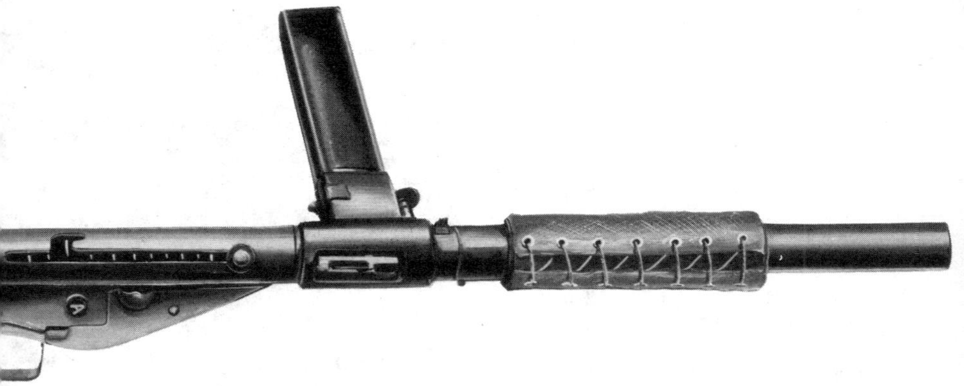

The Sten Gun Mark II. The name is derived from the first letters of the inventors' names (Sheppard and Tarpin) and the first letters of Enfield, where the gun was developed. A cheap and easily produced weapon, it was made in millions and was a valued tool of resistance forces all over Europe. In experienced hands it was surprisingly accurate and – legend notwithstanding – perfectly safe for the user. *Rate of fire* : 500/550 rounds per minute. *Magazine capacity* : 32 rounds, 9mm. *Effective range* : 80 yards. *Weight* : 6.62lbs. *Length* : 30 inches. *Muzzle velocity* : 1,280 feet per second ed to shoot at him. Kubiš then jumped on the cycle and rode fast down towards the city, almost blinded by pouring blood. The third man, Valčík, calmly left the place without being molested. When the staggering Heydrich reached the tram stop, he asked a Czech policeman who was standing among waiting passengers to telephone the office telling them about the attempt on his life. He then asked to be taken to hospital. At once the policeman stopped a passing van; the Protector was laid among boxes filled with shoe polish and driven to the Bulovka hospital not far from the tram stop. He did not seem to be seriously wounded, but was grimly determined to make the would-be assassins and the Czechs pay dearly for this indignity.

Immediately the most frantic and extensive search for the three men was launched. Everyone living in the area was arrested and interrogated. One tram passenger, an old woman, who was wounded in the blast, was kept in prison for six days and beaten up to admit that she was somehow connected with the assassination attempt. At 12.15 pm Frank telephoned Hitler who was furious to hear that Heydrich had had no escort with him. He peremptorily ordered Frank to take over from Heydrich, but to move nowhere without an escort, and even promised him an armoured car. He also ordered a reward of one million Reichsmarks for the capture of the assassins. Finally he asked Frank to shoot anyone connected with the attempt, and ordered him to arrest and execute 10,000 Czechs as a reprisal. After 5 pm the radio began to broadcast with terrifying regularity Frank's proclamation: 'As a consequence of the assassination attempt on the Acting Protector, SS-*Obergruppenführer* Heydrich, it is ordained:

Heydrich's damaged Mercedes shows the havoc caused by Kubiš's grenade attack

Despite the malfunction of Gabčík's
Sten gun the Reich Protector's car is
halted

The Junkers Ju 52/3m. The Ju 52 series must be, with the DC 3, the most famous transport aircraft developed before the Second World War. Originally designed as a single engined machine, it was later redesigned to take three radials, the original one in the nose, plus two more in the wings. During the war, the Luftwaffe used the Ju 52/3 as its maid of all work — trainer, transport, glider tug, paratroop dropper, emergency bomber, mine sweeper and general communications aircraft. *Engines :* Three BMW 132 radials, 830hp each. *Crew :* 3 plus up to 17 passengers. *Armament :* Up to four machine guns. *Speed :* 189mph. *Climb :* 19 minutes to 9,840 feet. *Ceiling :* 18,000 feet. *Range :* 930 miles. *Weight : empty/loaded :* 14,325/24,320lbs. *Span :* 95 feet 10 inches. *Length :* 62 feet

Article I According to paragraph one of the Protector's ordinance of 27th September 1941 martial law is proclaimed throughout the Protectorate of Bohemia and Moravia from this instant.

Article II According to paragraph two of the same ordinance all persons who have taken part in the assassination attempt as well as those who aid them, hide them or know their identity or place of hiding, and do not inform the authorities, are liable to be shot together with their families.

Article III This proclamation becomes effective by its broadcast. Prague, 27th May 1942, K H Frank, representing the Protector of Bohemia and Moravia.'

All the security organisations in the Czech provinces were alerted and telegraphed the news to Himmler. The latter confirmed Frank's telegram and approved all the measures taken so far. He added a small request of his own: Frank should execute one hundred of the intended 10,000 hostages the same night. Frank considered the situation in the Czech provinces so grave that early next day he took Heydrich's Junkers 52 and flew to Hitler's headquarters to report in person. He obviously saw the chance of advancing his own career through the crisis, but disappointment awaited him. After an interview with Hitler at which he made his recommendations as to how to tackle the situation, Frank was told that all the necessary decisions had already been taken. Hitler asked SS-*Oberstgruppenführer* and General of the Police, Kurt Daluege, to become Heydrich's provisional successor. Hitler consoled Frank that this was a provisional appointment and that he had not lost the Führer's confidence. Hitler also repeated his order for the instant execution of 10,000 Czechs, but Frank made alternative suggestions. First he wanted a monster search, then rewards for informers and only when these measures failed, large scale reprisals should be taken.

Below left : The car after the attack ; Heydrich died eight days later from blood poisoning. *Below : SS-Oberstgruppenführer* and General of Police Kurt Daluege, Heydrich's provisional successor

Müller, Chief of the Gestapo and active in the hunt for the assassins

Arthur Nebe, Chief of the Kripo. He took leave from Holland to help in the hunt

Hitler agreed to these modifications and gave a free hand to the *Staatssekretär*, who immediately flew back to Prague.

Throughout 28th May 1942 top security men from the Reich gathered in Prague to help in the search for the assailants. The Gestapo chief, Müller, arrived; A Nebe, the *Kripochief*, took leave from Holland to lend a hand; Heydrich's closest collaborators, Schellenberg and Kaltenbrunner, made their appearance. Two days later, the *Reichsführer* Himmler himself arrived, but this was already after the greatest search ever organised was completed. On 28th a curfew was imposed on Prague from 9pm to 6am and 4,500 security men joined by 2,400 Wehrmacht soldiers made a meticulous search of Prague. They arrested 541 people: 430 were subsequently released, 111 further interrogated and twenty-three suspects were kept in custody – among these was the wounded Zika, member of the communist central committee. All over Bohemia and Moravia some 450,000 security men and soldiers took part in the search; 4,750,000 Czechs were checked and 13,119 arrested. Also on the 28th the first executions took place: six people were sentenced to death (two of them women) and the sentences were carried out immediately. However, no one in any way connected with the assassination attempt was found or arrested.

Although the Germans knew the descriptions of the assassins and also found incriminating material, a Stengun, the second grenade, and the bicycle which Gabčík had abandoned, they were unable to trace the men. It was, however, certain that they were Czech agents from Britain parachuted into the Protectorate. The Gestapo had previously arrested several of them; it had in custody several others and even had one or two working for them. The search was concentrated on places and people who had provided hiding places or were in any way connected with these people. In fact the first reprisals taken in the form of executions were those of people who had sheltered parachutists in southern Bohemia. To avoid capture, all the men of Commandos 'Anthropoid', 'Silver A, B' and 'Zinc' in Prague, left their shelters in houses and hid in the crypt of the Orthodox Church in Ressel Street in the city centre. They were relatively safe,

Above : One of the bicycles left by the commandos after the assassination. *Below left :* The cap and raincoat left at the scene of the attack. *Below right :* One of the briefcases, also from the scene of the assassination

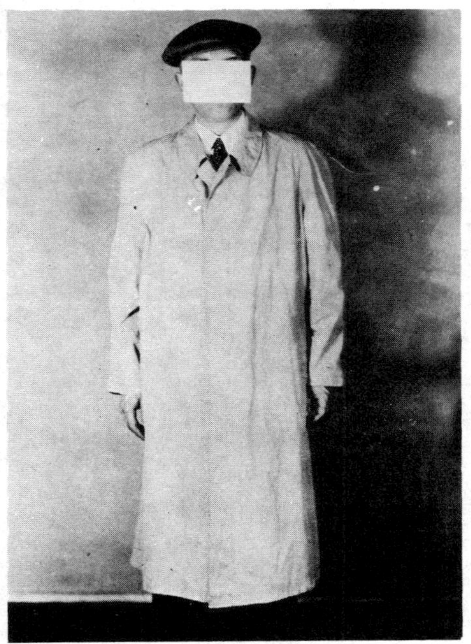

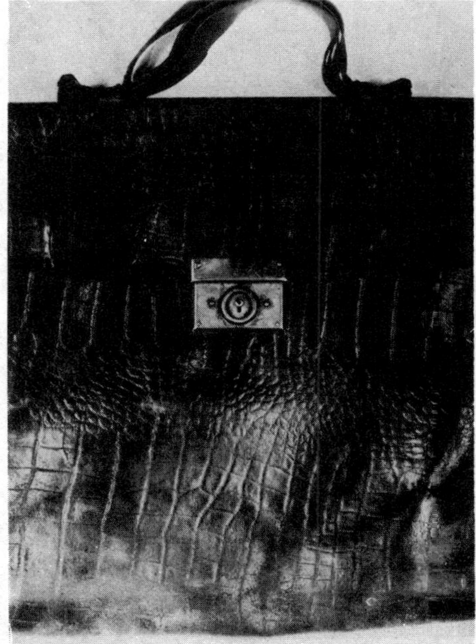

Heydrich's body is transferred
from the Bulovka hospital to Prague
Castle before shipment to Berlin.

Heydrich's funeral procession, Berlin, 9th June 1942

reasonably well provisioned by their friends, but hopelessly trapped, if discovered by the Germans. However, barring chance discovery, only betrayal could uncover them. In the meantime German investigations and reprisals followed a completely false lead.

On his arrival at the hospital Protector Heydrich had been examined by doctors. His wound looked superficial, but X-ray examination revealed impurities in the thorax and pancreatic gland, (possibly splinters of the grenade) and he had to be operated on. He tried to get his Berlin surgeon to attend him, but the emergency operation had to be performed by local doctors. It was successful: the impurities were removed from the patient, but shreds from his uniform caused blood poisoning. Transfusions were tried, but did not help. On 4th June 1942, in the absence of penicillin, the Security Chief of the Reich and Protector of the Czechs died.

Police investigations and reprisals went on unabated, but for a long time yielded no clues. Nonetheless, on 28th May the Gestapo had made a good guess when they connected Valčík, whom they had almost caught in March at Pardubice, with the assassination. The resistance and the parachutists were surprised to see

Valčík's photograph, name and description pasted on all the crossroads in Prague. Informers were promised a substantial reward, if they helped with the arrest. But the Gestapo did not know that Valčík actually took part in the attempt, they were simply guessing.

They also had the bicycles, briefcases and a cap and raincoat left behind by Gabčík and Kubiš. All of them were exhibited in the Bata shop window in Wenceslas Square and people who would identify them were promised rewards. Independently the police tried to trace the original owner of the raincoat; but none of these efforts led to any significant discoveries.

The clues found near the scene are exhibited in the window of the Bata shop in Wenceslas Square, Prague

Between 28th May and 9th June 1942 German courts martial sentenced some 1,800 Czechs to death, and the sentences were immediately carried out. Long lists of victims, against whom nothing could be proved, were pasted daily in the streets and published in newspapers.

The Acting Protector Heydrich died on 4th June in Prague: five days later he was buried in Berlin. Hitler, Himmler and Frank attended the funeral; the decision to destroy Lidice was taken immediately after the funeral.

Heydrich's funeral. Front row, left to right : Daluege, Heydrich's sons, Heinz Heydrich, Himmler, Göring and Hitler. Ley, Frick, Goebbels and Bormann are behind

Heydrich's funeral. Hitler delivers an oration

Lidice

The sequence of events leading up to the destruction of Lidice was unspectacular. It started inconspicuously in Slany, a small town in central Bohemia. On 3rd June 1942 the mayor of Slaný, a director of the local battery factory, J Pála, was sorting out his mail, when he came across a letter addressed to one of his women workers. He opened it and read: 'Dear Ann, forgive me for writing so late and perhaps you will understand, for you know I have plenty of worries. What I wanted to do, I did. On that fateful night I slept somewhere at Čabarny. I am all right, hope to see you this week and then we shall never see each other again. Milan.'

Pála's nerves were obviously on edge and the mysterious letter frightened him terribly. Instead of passing it on to the woman or destroying it, since he thought it suspicious, he telephoned the local Czech gendarmerie that he had intercepted a very important letter. Gendarme Vybíral was then sent to Pála to collect the communication. But after reading it he was more puzzled than terrified, for he thought it was a simple love letter. However, Pála insisted that the letter must have been written by one of the assassins of the Protector, and gave the gendarme the name and address of the woman it was sent to. Miss Ann Marusczáková was not at work on that day, but ill at home. On the way back to the police station Vybíral thought

Lidice before the war

of driving to Marusczáková's home and warning her, but his motorcycle was out of order and he could not do so. He thus might have saved the girl and possibly even Lidice, but it was not to be so. After reading the letter, his superior also reacted rather luke-warmly, but when told of Pála's insistence he rang up the Gestapo branch at Kladno and promised to deliver the letter within an hour. Together with gendarme Šmaha he rode by car to Kladno where investigations began immediately.

The deputy chief of the Kladno Gestapo, T Thomsen, had the letter translated and then sent his interpreter, together with the Czech gendarme, to Holous, a village not far from Lidice, to search Marusczáková's home and arrest her. The search yielded nothing, but the girl was arrested all the same and taken to Kladno, where her interrogation was conducted by the chief, Wiesmann, his deputy Thomsen and interpreter Fekl. The girl's story was clear and straight-forward: not long ago she had made the acquaintance of a young man whom she had met several times since. He always arrived on a bicycle which had a registration number of the Prague iron works at Kladno. Once the young man asked her whether she had friends or relations at Lidice and when she told him she had a friend there, he asked her to convey greetings to the family Horák, especially to their son, Joseph. From this Marusczáková deduced that he was Joseph Horák himself, and since he had escaped to Britain in 1939, he must have been one of the parachutists, possibly even one of the assassins. The innocence of this admission shocked even the cynical Gestapo men who must have smelled an error somewhere. When the girl was shown photographs of several parachutists who were probably connected with the attempt, she did not recognise her young man among them. Despite the contradictions, the Gestapo followed up this lead and telephoned the Iron Works to find out to whom the bicycle in question belonged.

Wiesmann also wanted to visit this village, Lidice, for the Gestapo had heard of it from previous cases. But by pronouncing the word in the German fashion, he was taken by the gendarmes to another village, Litice. There Wiesmann asked the mayor whether he had the family Horák in the village; the mayor searched his files but there was no trace of the Horáks. Later, passing through another village, Buštěhrad, Fekl, who spoke Czech, discovered that Lidice was not far away. The Buštěhrad gendarmerie told Fekl that several families with the surname Horák lived at Lidice, but that only one of them had a young son whose whereabouts were unknown. This fact was not only known to the gendarmes but also to the Gestapo. Josef Horák disappeared in 1939 and as Lieutenant of the Czechoslovak Air Force together with Josef Stříbrny, also a pilot and native of Lidice, had joined the RAF in Britain. When, however, Fekl intimated that Horák was an accomplice in the assassination of Heydrich the Buštěhrad gendarmes told him this was absolute nonsense: no one had heard of Horák since 1939 and Marusczáková's description did not fit him. Nevertheless Fekl telephoned Thomsen and reported on his finding. Thomsen took over further investigation and alerted security forces at Kladno, Slaný and even in Prague for a night search of Lidice.

The Prague Headquarters sent four Gestapo members to join the Kladno branch led by Wiesmann, and also two units of the *Schutzpolizei*. The village of Lidice and Čabarny, a nearby hamlet with a few houses, were ringed off. Gestapo officials went first to Čabarny. All the houses were thoroughly searched and inhabitants asked whether any strangers had slept in the hamlet recently. But the search and interrogation at Čabarny failed to produce anything remotely suspicious. Despite this disappointment,

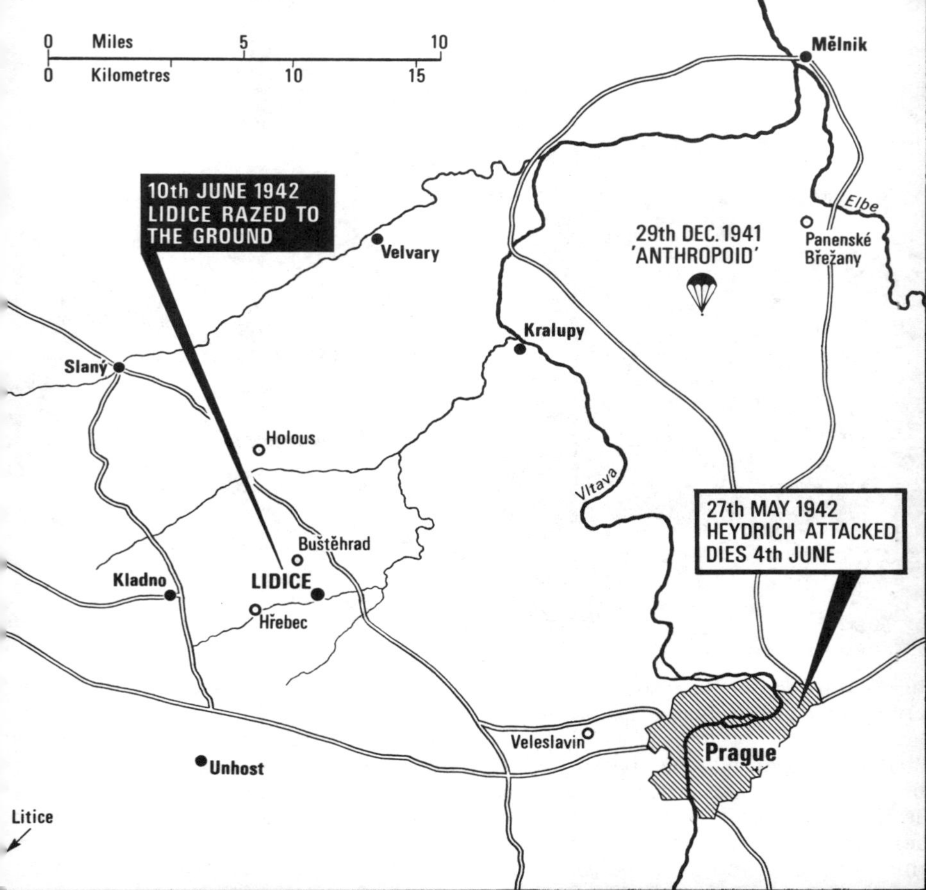

The events leading up to the destruction of Lidice

**The church and the old granary
in the centre of the village**

Wiesmann ordered the arrest of all the men and had them transported to his Kladno headquarters. Some thirty men were loaded into two coaches which the Gestapo brought along for the operation. Afterwards the Gestapo drove off to nearby Lidice which was surrounded by the *Schutzpolizei* with orders to let anyone in, but no one out. As most of the houses stood alongside the road which ran through the village, the Gestapo men split into two groups and carried out house to house searches. Particular attention was paid to the farms inhabited by the Horáks and Stříbrnýs. The Germans still hoped that the two missing Lidice men were hiding at home after being parachuted into Czechoslovakia, and taking part in the assassination. But even these searches and interrogations proved fruitless, with one exception: the Gestapo uncovered several photographs of Horák and Stříbný. These were, apparently, sufficient excuse for the wholesale arrest of the two families. Altogether fifteen persons were taken to the Kladno Gestapo for further interrogation. With the operation concluded, the Gestapo men returned to Kladno and began interrogating those arrested at Čabarny and the families of the missing men.

The interrogation was conducted intensively by the Gestapo teams led by Thomsen. However, despite the forceful methods employed the men admitted nothing. One by one they were released and sent home. But the members of the two Lidice families, although they also continued to repeat to the Gestapo that the two young men had left home in 1939, and no one had heard from them since, were kept in custody. The pretext for detention was Marusczáková, who when confronted with all the photographs collected at Lidice, identified Lieutenant Horák as the young man she had been out with.

In the meantime the Gestapo ar-

76

rested three workers from the Prague Iron Works at Kladno, whose bicycles and registration numbers corresponded to the description given by Maruszáková. They were taken to the headquarters for confrontation with her. She then identified one of them as the man who wrote the letter to her and who had asked her to convey a message to the Horák family. The young worker, V Říha, was immediately arrested and interrogated, while the other two were released. He confessed that he had asked Maruszáková to pass on the message, because he once met young Horák and had been requested to do so. This was an obvious invention, for the two Lidice men were pilots serving in the Air Force in England and it was highly unlikely that trained pilots would be used for missions of assassination as the Gestapo imagined. It is also possible that this confession was never made: both Maruszáková and Říha were sent, after the destruction of Lidice, to concentration camps at Mauthausen and Mühlhausen, where they both died before the end of the war. It is quite possible, though it cannot be proved, that the Gestapo thought that this was the only way of capturing the assassins. In the absence of any concrete proof of Horák's guilt, the Gestapo decided to use the 'confession' of the innocent young couple as an excuse to commit one of the worst atrocities of the war at Lidice.

The final decisions and recommendations concerning the fate of the village were made by Karel Hermann Frank, who after Heydrich's death was the most powerful man in the Czech provinces. In his decision he was certainly not guided by reason or legal evidence. For him the destruction of Lidice was an act of reprisal. On Heydrich's death Frank wrote in the Nazi newspaper, *Völkischer Beobachter*: 'The criminal forces in the Czech nation, hostile to the German Reich, will be rooted out. As in the early hours of 4th June 1942 the young

Horst Böhm, Security Police Chief, claimed by Frank to have given him the order for the destruction of Lidice

and passionate life of Reinhard Heydrich ebbed away, I and the SS *Oberstgruppenführer* Daluege, who were at the death bed, swore to each other that we would carry out the task of our comrade. His instructions would be followed.' On 9th June 1942 Heydrich was buried in Berlin with all military pomp and honour and shortly after the funeral Frank made clear the meaning of his vow. Later, when the war was over Frank was to claim that the destruction of Lidice was accomplished on Hitler's direct order. Frank was unable to remember any precise details but claimed that he had been given the order by the security police chief, Böhm, on his return from Berlin, whence he went with Heydrich's two children to attend the funeral. Frank further claimed that the investigation of this particular case was confined to a special commission, which afterwards reported to Hitler directly; thus, Hitler's brutal order, based on the findings and recommendations of this commission, was entirely his own.

We shall probably never know with certainty what Frank recommended to Hitler. However, on the day of Heydrich's funeral, the Gestapo chief in Prague, Horst Böhm, typed out the

Karl Hermann Frank, probable originator of the plan to make an example of Lidice

following telephone message: 'On 9th June 1942 at 19.45 *Gruppenführer* Frank telephoned after an interview with Hitler and told me to deal with the commune of Lidice in the following manner:

1 All men to be executed by shooting.
2 All women to be sent into concentration camps.
3 Children are to be concentrated, those capable of being Germanised, are to be sent to SS families in Germany and the rest elsewhere.
4 The commune is to be burnt down and levelled to the ground.'

On 12th June Frank countersigned this order, but by then the destruction had been carried out. On 10th June, after his return from Berlin, Frank ordered the terrified members of the Czech government to appear before him and read out to them his instructions about Lidice. At this audience he also uttered the words: '*Ich habe angeordnet*' (I have ordered it), which probably meant that he had given Hitler the idea for the barbarous act.

Thomsen interrogated the Horáks and Stříbrnýs again and confronted them with Říha's story; but they all denied any knowledge of the whereabouts of Lieutenant Horák. Wies-

mann must have known that Říha and Marusczáková were exaggerating or lying, but chose to believe them and blamed the Lidice families. Once he had made up his mind, he passed the files and his recommendations on to Prague headquarters and demanded rigorous action. The Gestapo and all the security services were in a difficult position in their hunt for the assassins. So far their efforts had proved utterly fruitless; countless hostages and many innocent people had been executed, but the real culprits were still at large. Almost in despair, the Germans turned to this insignificant episode and rather implausible line of investigation, and decided to use it to commit one of the most terrible atrocities of the war. A confused love affair and photographs of two missing men became the thin

basis for the outrage. (Ríha was married and this is probably why he acted so mysteriously and perhaps lied.)

Obviously the Gestapo men on the spot knew nothing of the great decisions that were made in Berlin, based on their Slaný case. But they were full of expectation when on 9th June they were all ordered to dress in uniform and be ready for action. Wiesmann requisitioned a lorry on which two barrels of petrol were loaded. At 10pm everyone gathered in the courtyard; two units of the *Schutzpolizei* joined the Gestapo. Wiesmann who up to that time had been in conference with Thomsen, Czech gendarmerie commander at Kladno, Vít, and his Prague superior, SS-*Standartenführer*, Dr Geschke, came out to issue his final instructions. The men were divided into groups and each group was given a task to perform. The general order was to search all houses in Lidice; particular orders were to gather all men above fourteen years of age in the courtyard of the Horák farm, and all women and children in the local school. All the inhabitants were to be ordered to take with them their valuables and savings books. Shortly after 10pm the Germans involved in the operation set out by cars for the village. When the column of cars, lorries and coaches reached Buštěhrad, some thirty Gestapo officials occupied the gendarmerie and telephoned Prague. The Czech commander overheard this conversation: '*Auf Befehl des Führers wird die Gemeinde Liditz von Frauen und Kin-*

Lidice burns

dern evakuiert, die Männer von 16 fahren ab auf der Stelle erschossen und zum Schluss die Gemeinde abgebrannt.' (On the Führer's order the women and children will be evacuated from Lidice, men over sixteen shot on the spot and the village subsequently burnt.) The great secret was out, but the Czech gendarmes were now powerless even to warn the poor villagers. Lidice was by then surrounded by the security troops. The Gestapo cars and top security personnel drove up to the village, parked their cars at the first house and walked to the main square. In the presence of Horst Böhme, SS-*Standartenführer* and chief of the Prague Gestapo, Dr Geschke, of the security police in Prague, leading members of the Kladno Gestapo and security services as well as Lieutenant-Colonel Vít, commander of the Czech gendarmerie, Wiesmann formally read out the order: *'Führerbefehl: Liditz wird dem Erdboden gleichgemacht und die Bevölkerung erschossen.'* (Lidice will be flattened and the population shot. Führer's order.)

The operation proceeded smoothly. Everything was well planned, methodically prepared and executed without fuss. At first the mayor of Lidice was taken to a house and handed over communal petty cash, accounts, savings and all the papers pertaining to the property of the village. German agricultural experts were then called in to confiscate the cattle, agricultural machinery, food reserves and stores. After these preliminaries the Gestapo and special security groups went into action proper and a hunt for the men started. The Gestapo base was Horák's orchard: from there groups of four to five security men filed out to every house in the village, woke up its inhabitants and sorted them out. Men went with their escorts back to the orchard, while women and children were pushed into the school.

Agricultural machinery is removed from Lidice prior to the levelling

Lidice's church, seen from the ruins of an inn

Women were told to take all their valuables with them and on arriving at the school the Gestapo confiscated them: money, savings books, jewels and silver were thrown into two suitcases and subsequently taken to Kladno Gestapo HQ where they disappeared without a trace.

The arrests and sorting out of the men were conducted in the most methodical fashion. The mayor was asked to produce the communal register and all the men over sixteen years were checked against it. Despite this administrative thoroughness eleven men could not be accounted for when the counting and checking had been accomplished. The mayor, however, was able to enlighten the Gestapo about the missing men: they were on the night shift at Kladno and would be returning in the morning. As it happened these men did try to return to the village, but seeing the village surrounded, nine returned to Kladno and two hid in the forest nearby. A total of 173 men were under arrest in the cellar and barn of Horák's farm, and at this stage none of them had any idea of their subsequent fate. At dawn the Gestapo lorry with the barrels of petrol arrived and was stationed in the village square: security men then filled smaller receptacles with petrol and took them to all the houses. Afterwards the lorry drove round the village and was reloaded with any useful possessions that could be found – sewing machines, perambulators, bicycles and motorcycles and various pieces of furniture which were later appropriated by members of the Kladno Gestapo. Even though the operation was extremely well organised, it nonetheless caused a terrible commotion in the village. One member of the *Schnellkomando* declared subsequently: 'My nerves were on edge. Women wailed like mad, children howled, dogs barked, the cattle mooed, chickens were flying all over the place . . .' On 10th June at seven o'clock in the morning, the *Staatssekretär*, K H Frank, arrived with several senior SS officers. After the war he described his visit to Lidice to his interrogators: 'On my return from Berlin, on 10th June 1942, I drove to Lidice to see on the spot how Hitler's orders were carried out. I can only recall that I saw the village in flames, houses in ruin and that I did not dare to penetrate into the village itself. It was on the edge of the village that Böhme reported on the execution of Hitler's order and the shooting of Lidice men.

'I also recall that I saw a number of corpses behind a house and noticed heaps of earth. At this time several explosions occurred: the officer of the security detachment explained that the fire probably reached munitions or explosives. Because of these explosions I hesistated to go farther into the burning village and apart from this, I cannot recall any other impression of this visit. I stayed at Lidice only very shortly and returned to Prague . . . perhaps on 11th June I went to Lidice for the second time with a large number of other people. On the spot we began to deal with the destruction of the village which was to be carried out by the pioneers and its levelling to the ground which was to be performed by the Reich labour service. For Hitler's order literally meant that the village had to be levelled to the ground . . . Much later I went to Lidice for the third time, on the invitation of the labour leader when Lidice was almost levelled out.'

In his version Frank obviously confused several of his visits. In fact his arrival on the 10th was the signal for the final tragedy: he formally repeated Hitler's order and only then did the execution squads go into action. Women and children were taken out of the school and loaded into the prepared coaches which drove them off to Kladno. They were not allowed to see their menfolk and make their farewells. Mercifully in the last moment they were joined by several boys who were under sixteen and were originally taken to Horák's farm. As

soon as the coaches disappeared, orders were given to burn the village: house after house was set on fire until the whole place was in flames. Before the village church was set ablaze a particularly horrible episode took place. The Gestapo chief, Böhme, was evidently interested in the church; he hoped to confiscate all the precious vessels and antique ornaments. His men collected all that was of any value and put it into a box. They put the historical records from the church into another box and took them away. The old parish priest, Father Štemberk, aged seventy-three, who was being taken to Horák's farm witnessed the plundering of his church by the security men. As he passed one of the Gestapo men he appealed to him not to desecrate his church; he was brutally assaulted for his pains and knocked down onto the road with a blow. Several other security men joined in abusing and kicking the old man in the dust.

At Horák's farm the most methodic-

The destruction continues, efficient and relentless

al preparations for the executions were started. All the mattresses from the farm and surrounding houses were taken to the large barn at the end of the orchard and placed standing against one of the walls. A thirty-men-strong execution squad was ready, together with reserves in case anyone felt faint. Three squad men would shoot at the Lidice men, who were to be brought in for execution by firing in batches of ten. The scene was grotesque: the burning village in the background and ten innocent men, without any hint of the impending doom, brought forward to face death. No sentence was read out to them, no formality observed; their eyes were not bound, but, nonetheless, they faced their executioners with calm and dignity. The first ten lined up very quietly; Böhme made no noise but only nodded. The officer in charge of the squad gave a signal

'On the Führer's order men over
sixteen will be shot on the spot'

with his sabre and the first salvo killed the civilians. The squad NCO walked up to the dead and fired a shot from his revolver into every head to make doubly sure. The squad then re-loaded and in ten minutes the next batch came. The dead remained where they fell: the next ten simply placed themselves one step in front of them. The ghastly proceedings were then repeated. After fifty executions the squad of the Schutzpolizei took a break and Schnapps was served to steady their nerves. Only three refused to go on and were replaced by reserve men.

The executions were then resumed. The ten victims stood like silent statues, petrified in front of their lifeless friends and relations. No one uttered a word. Father Štemberk spoke to them all before they were taken out, prayed with them, gave them last absolutions and blessed them. One of the squad laughed about it: '*Der Pfaffe hat das gut gemacht. Durch sein Beten und Segnungen hat er die Leute dazu gebracht, dass sie wie die Schafe zur Hinrichtung gegangen sind.*' (The old priest did it well. With his prayer and blessing he made the men go to their execution like sheep.) In the sixth or seventh group one young man, F Kubík, suddenly and unexpectedly asked the commanding officer: 'Gentlemen, do tell us what you want to know and we shall tell you what we can.' The officer hesitated, turned towards the Gestapo men, but when they failed to react to this desperate appeal, moved his sabre and all were mowed down. But young Kubík was only wounded and writhed in agony on the ground. Several men swiftly finished him off with revolvers.

Another unplanned commotion broke out in the cellar. Despite Fr Štemberk's encouragements one man tried to cheat the executioners by committing suicide. With a penknife he cut the arteries in the neck but, still alive, he was snatched up by the guards and shot either in the cellar or outside in the orchard. It is not known when the priest was executed, but it seems he was among the last to die. During that morning of 10th June 1942, 173 men perished in the orchard of the Horák family's farm. By noon seventeen rows of corpses in bloody clothes, with shattered skulls, brains and guts spilling out, lay on the ground in batches of ten. With the executions completed, gold rings were taken off the dead and gold teeth gouged out. The first task was completed; the remaining men, some eleven of them, were still to be traced and brought before the executioners. The Horáks and Stříbnýs would die last.

At the end of their task, the execution squad was completely drunk. Their nerves had given way and many had to be sent out of the village. Most of the Gestapo and security men also left Lidice for Kladno and Prague. The immediate task had been carried out; the men were dead, the houses burning. Only a chain of guards was left behind round the scene of destruction, to prevent anyone from entering the devastated commune.

But outside Lidice the Germans continued their hunt for the missing men and their inhuman treatment of the women and children. Nine men who returned to the iron works at Kladno were easily traced: the German factory guard arrested them and took them to the Kladno Gestapo. They were executed in Prague together with the Horáks and Stříbnýs. The two who tried to escape by hiding in a forest were forced by hunger after two days to ask a Czech forester to bring them food. Trustingly they even gave him their ration coupons. The forester, who had guessed that they were the wanted Lidice men, promised everything, but as soon as he got home, informed the Gestapo. Czech gendarmes were then ordered to comb the woods and capture the fugitives. These two were also taken to Prague and executed. Ironically, the members of the

Some of the children from the village ; out of 104 taken to Germany only sixteen were traced and repatriated to Czechoslovakia

Only three of this group of Lidice's
second-year elementary schoolchildren
were returned to Czechoslovakia after
the war

**Antonie Černá and Božena Kavarovská,
two of the Lidice women to return home**

Horák and Stříbrny families were not put to death in their native village, but in Prague and in due form: they were sentenced by a court martial and the sentences were immediately carried out.

At Kladno, in the afternoon, the Gestapo concentrated all the Lidice women and children in the local grammar school and made a register of them. 185 women were to be sent to the concentration camp at Ravensbrück; seven women who had children under one year were at first to be sent to the Terezín camp and then finally to Ravensbrück. Four pregnant women, one of them a sister of Flight-Lieutenant Horák, were taken to a clinic in Prague. Immediately after their confinement they were shipped to Ravensbrück without their children.

The registration and sorting out of the women took almost two days. All this time the women and children knew nothing of what had happened in the village. Neither did they know what fate was in store for them. From the hints around them they could have guessed, but all was so confused that none did. During the second day several SS officers arrived at Kladno, visited the school and chose two girls and a boy for the 'Germanisation' experiment in German families.

Stories told later by the survivors

you had fifty fully armed SS men on the one hand, and us, defenceless terrified weak women on the other. Slowly the SS called the names of the children, who either came on their own or were taken by force from their mothers. The piercing cries of the children were terrible: "don't let me go, Mummy", "Please don't cry . . . I'll come back" . . . Hardly any of us could understand all this; most of us fell down on the straw crying in despair.' The children's stories are pathetic but on the whole matter of fact; they were so numb with terror that they forgot fear: 'They took us to Kladno, to the grammar school. I had never been to Kladno before and never seen such a big town. The houses were as large as our church and the school, where they took us, was also immense. We were taken to the gym. Then some other people joined us and mothers told us they were the Gestapo. They were asking questions all the time, looked into our eyes and at our hair. They wrote down a lot and then left us. Some other men brought us coffee and dry bread. For dinner we had soup and potatoes, the same in the evening. That day, it was Wednesday, no one knew that they had shot all our fathers and grandfathers. We thought, and our mothers too, that we would see them again. The night came, but we could hear crying all the time so we hardly slept. I slept a while and Mother sat next to me . . . The whole of Thursday passed with nothing much happening: again black coffee and for dinner potatoes. From time to time someone came and wanted to know something, but our mothers were tired and we, too. We could not play and in any case no one felt like it.

'On Friday evening many men came into the gym. They put us on one side and mothers on another . . . Apparently they would go somewhere by train and we would follow by coach. But our mothers did not believe it and did not want to let us go. They held us fast and the men in uniform had plenty of trouble separating us. In the end they

are terrifying: 'We were all driven into the school's gymnasium and slept on the floor on which some straw had been scattered to soften it. After three days which were filled with the cries of children and black despair of the mothers, some fifty SS men arrived in the gymnasium. One of them said that we would all go to a concentration camp. When we asked what happened to our men he answered that they would also go to a concentration camp. The children would also follow them, but separately, in greater comfort. We shall therefore leave first . . . But we could not believe anything . . . mothers took their children into their arms and held them tight to protect them with their own bodies. However,

173 men were executed in the orchard
of the Horák farm

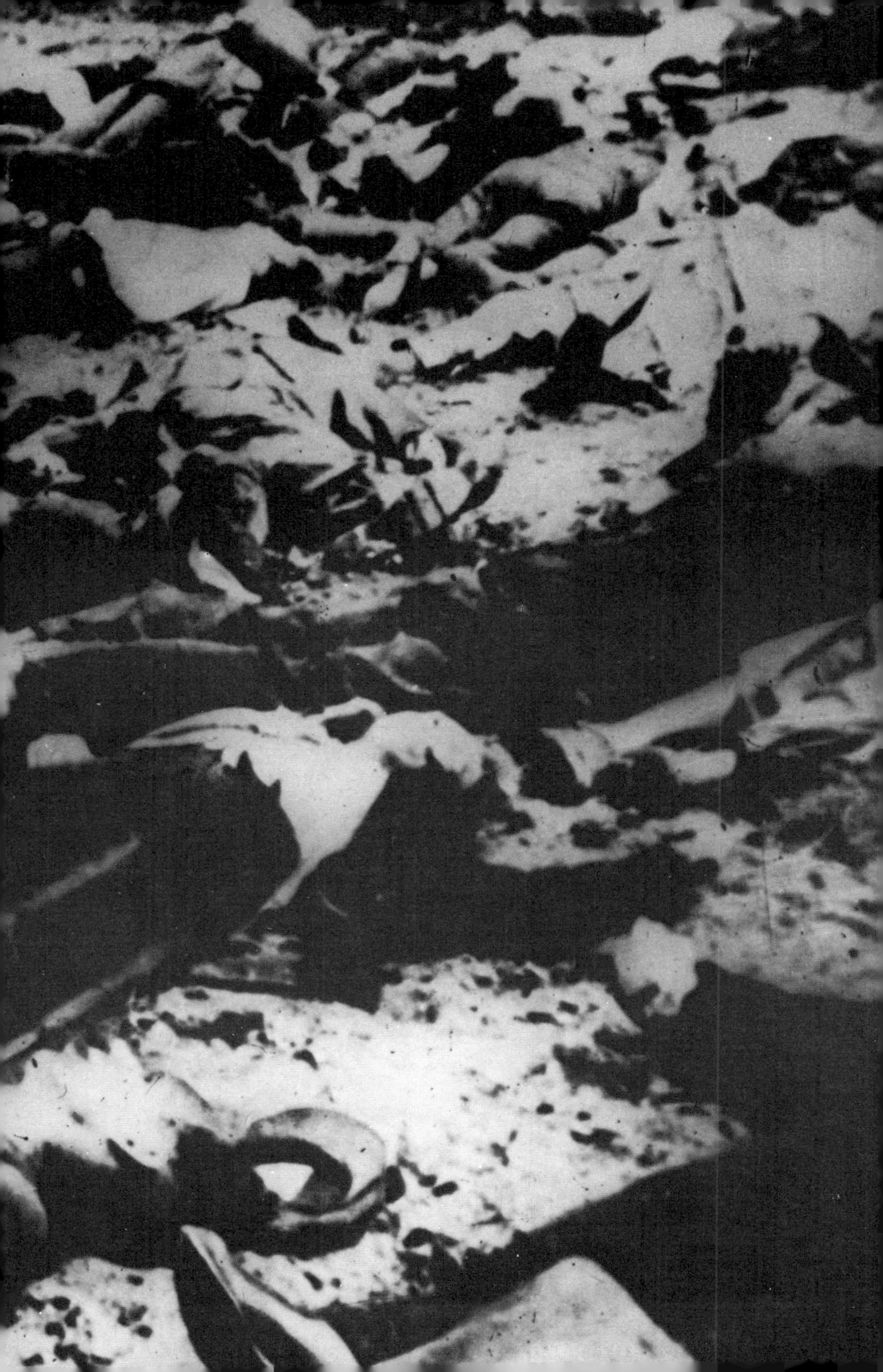

Umwandererzentralstelle
L.:Kr./En.VIII/26 Tgb.-Nr.6113/42   Litzmannstadt, den 2o.Juni 1942

Geheime Staatspolizei — Staatspolizeistelle Litzmannstadt

Nachrichten-Uebermittlung

Aufgenommen				Raum für Eingangsstempel	Befördert			
Zeit	Tag	Monat	Jahr		Zeit	Tag	Monat	Jahr
von		durch			an		durch	

Verzögerungsvermerk

N.-Ü. Nr. 06167 | Telegramm — Funkspruch — Fernschreiben
Fernspruch

F e r n s c h r e i b e n

An das
Reichssicherheitshauptamt
- Referat IV B 4 -
z.Hd.SS-Obersturmbannführer E i c h m a n n
B e r l i n
Kurfürstenstraße 115/116

Betr.: Überstellung von 88 tschechischen Kindern aus
       der Gemeinde Liditz nach Litzmannstadt.
Vorg.: Rücksprache mit SS-Ostubaf.Eichmann.

Am 13.6.1942 sind hier 88 tschechische Kinder aus
der obengenannten Gemeinde eingetroffen. Angemeldet
war dieser Transport vom Befehlshaber der Sicherheitspolizei und des SD, Prag. Das FS war gezeichnet von
SS-Obersturmbannführer F i s c h e r .

In einem FS vom 17.6.1942 habe ich den Befehlshaber
der Sipo u.d.SD gebeten, bei IV B 4 zu klären, was
mit den tschechischen Kindern zu geschehen hat. Vor
RuS sind in der Zwischenzeit 7 Kinder als rückdeutschungs-
fähig befunden worden.

Nachdem ich weder von IV B 4 noch vom Befehlshaber
der Sipo u.d.SD über die Weiterverwendung der Kinder
Nachricht habe und die Kinder ohne Gepäck hierher über-
stellt worden sind, bitte ich dringend, über die Weiterverwendung der Kinder zu verfügen.

(K r u m e y)
SS-Obersturmbannführer

The desecrated graveyard at Lidice

managed, because there were so many of them. From then on I could not see my mother. I only managed to shout to her not to be afraid, that I would not fall out of the bus and would hold myself firmly . . . but then the SS pulled out their revolvers, fired up into the ceiling so that we felt afraid. In one room they put round our necks a label with our names and numbers; we boys wanted to be brave and not to cry to set our girls an example. But in the end we also cried.'

On Friday 12th June the women were separated from their children to be taken to the camps. The farewells were heartrending. A Czech gendarme on guard duty outside the school, described the scene: 'We shall never forget that evening. At the moment when, in the school, the children were separated from their mothers a terrible wail went up; the crying children were taken to one of the classrooms on the first floor. At first we heard the crying and wailing of the children who had lost their fathers and were now losing their mothers. Those moments were heartbreaking. The Kladno citizens living in the houses near the school were not allowed even to look out through their windows. At 8pm two large coaches arrived at the school driven by German drivers . . . In the school building the SS and Gestapo were sorting out the women and children. Czech gendarmes were on duty in the corridors; the *Schupo* (*Schutzpolizei*) in the court yard. The women were taken away first, in large lorries covered with canvas. They were seated facing the guards armed to their teeth. Every lorry had at least four SS or policemen. The women looked pale, but behaved calmly, for they had no idea of what happened to their menfolk and youths, and were only upset by the farewells with their children. They stared expressionless in front of them. The file of seventeen lorries struck us as a funeral procession for

The Lidice schoolhouse, fired by the Germans during the destruction of the village

living victims. Then came the children's turn. Three of them, a boy and two girls were taken away to Prague by a grey Red Cross car; two German women in Red Cross uniform and a German driver accompanied them. Then the two coaches drew up in front of the main entrance. The first coach was filled with forty-six children, several Red Cross women and three Czech mothers probably mothers of the youngest children. Forty-eight children went into the second coach with the same number of Red Cross personnel. The children were taken down from the classroom under heavy guard. The guards remained standing round the entrance, watching carefully every movement of the defenceless creatures. These were very young children, almost babies. They were carrying small parcels (the Gestapo men arrested after the end of the war claimed that the children were given toys and sweets not to cry) holding their elder brothers or sisters by the other hand.' The coaches disappeared for ever and the children proved untraceable after the war. The last indications of their being alive were postcards written from a children's camp at Gneisenau.

While the women and children were disposed of, the Kladno Gestapo rechecked the registers of men. Despite all precautions, one Lidice man, shot in the orchard of Horák's farm, could not be identified. Wiesmann therefore ordered that all the corpses should again be searched and all the material found on them be brought to the Kladno Gestapo. Identity cards found on the dead were checked again against the registers, but the unknown man was not identified. It was thought that he was a farmhand who had

arrived at Lidice on 9th June and had not yet been entered on the register. After the slaughter of all the living, no one could identify this hapless victim. Although looting was strictly forbidden, all the valuables disappeared most mysteriously. When, shortly afterwards, Wiesmann was transferred to Warsaw, his property was evaluated at 10,000,000 Crowns: he had owned nothing when he arrived at Kladno.

On 11th June 1942 the burial of the massacred victims took place; a group of thirty Jewish prisoners from the Terezín camp drove in lorries to Lidice with a barrel of lime and SS guards. One of the survivers described the scene: 'They brought us on a lorry, together with lime and shovels and spades, as well as pickaxes. After a long drive they changed our guards and shortly afterwards we suddenly arrived near a burning village. Then we turned left and walked across a courtyard to an orchard where I remember seeing patches of potatoes and vegetables . . . when we came nearer, we stopped shocked – in front of us lay a heap of corpses in irregular rows.

'The German commanding officer and Dr Seidl, commander of the Terezín camp, approached the dead and Seidel pointed at the corpse of a tall strong man with a light blue vest on. Then he bent down, took a small dark handbag from the body, from which he extracted a packet of banknotes and put them into his own breast pocket. After this Seidel took one of the pickaxes and marked the mass grave which was to be dug up some ten metres from the dead bodies. It was to be four metres deep, and had to be ready by 10pm the same evening, else we would see what would happen to us. The first half metre was easy, but then we struck clay soil and slowed down. The SS guard began to

Nazi film unit sets up its camera before it was refused permission to shoot

beat us and we had to go on digging without a break or food. When Seidel arrived at 10pm hardly one metre was dug; he stopped the work and lined us up for a rollcall. We were then divided into groups of four and ordered to collect wood in the village. Under strict guard we had to go round breaking down doors, fences and heaped them near the grave. The guards poured some petrol on the wood, lit it and in the light of the flames, with the corpses clearly illuminated, we had to go on digging.

'The elderly and ill among us could hardly go on but were forced to by the beating and kicking of the SS guard. When we managed to dig out about two metres, Seidl arrived again, pointed to the burning pile and ordered us to collect some more wood. We had to go round collecting wardrobes, mattresses; the pile burst into flames again and without any food or drink we had to continue digging until noon the next day. Round about twelve o'clock, the Gestapo man Gunther came with a group of high ranking officers and a tall man, whom everybody called Frank. They were all amused, joked about the dead and we felt petrified. It must have been lunchtime, for the Gestapo men killed several hens and geese and started boiling them. Then Seidel came again to measure the grave which was exactly three metres deep.

'In the meantime a group of the Kladno Gestapo arrived and we overheard them saying that they were going to bring the women back to Lidice so that they could take farewell of their dead men. We were then ordered to stop digging and were waiting to see what would happen if the Gestapo carried out their intentions. But then another group of people arrived with film cameras and passes on their lapels, and they wanted to film the macabre scene. However. Seidel forbade it and ordered us to start carrying the corpses into the mass grave. We were ordered to take their boots off and empty their pockets of money,

valuables and cigarettes. "If anyone steals anything, he will be shot", Seidl added. Hesitatingly we approached the corpses: almost everyone had a small parcel of food on him. "You can have the food" Seidl offered, but although we were dead hungry, no one touched anything.

'Thus I saw five extremely young boys, almost babies, a white-haired priest, a shrunk old man and a policeman in his uniform. Everyone had a bullet in his heart, head and a hole under the chin. We also found a number of people with split skulls, formless faces, deformed by boots, a man with severed fingers and two men whose arms were torn out of the joints. All the corpses still had terrified expressions on their faces, eyes bulging out: one dead man had his hands clasped together in prayer, another was half burnt. We had to undress them and put their clothes in a heap; Seidl then stuffed them in sacks. The corpses were put into the grave sideways in three rows. The corpses that could not be laid out in this way, were thrown on top of the rows. When we finished the job, one of the policemen tried to call a dog to the grave, but the animal became terrified and attempted to run away howling. The policeman shot him dead and had us throw this body among the corpses. Another stray dog was killed near the church which was being mined together with the school building: the second dog was also thrown among the human corpses. We then had another break and towards the evening we were ordered to open the barrel of lime and spread the lime all over the corpses. As we were doing this, it started to rain, but we had to continue our work, until the soil was heaped on top of the corpses in the mass grave. It grew dark and before we could finish the task, we were suddenly called off and had to line up for departure to our camp. One of our lorries was loaded with cattle and poultry and we were squeezed onto the other. After thirty-six hours of ter-

German officers inspect the ruins prior to carrying out Hitler's orders that Lidice be levelled to the ground

Some 84,000 metres of soil and rubble
had to be moved and levelled out

The Reich Labour Service continues
the work at Lidice

German troops pose during the demolition of Lidice

rible labour without food or drink we were shipped back to Terezín.'

On 13th June 1942 at 3am another group of Jewish prisoners left Terezín for Lidice, presumably to complete the job. Another eyewitness' story of the desolation in the village survives: 'We passed through Buštěhrad towards Prague. There we met several lorries fully loaded with furniture, sewing machines, agricultural implements, perambulators. The road was patrolled by Czech gendarmes. We went downhill into Lidice which was full of the hated uniforms. A group of SS men came up to us and took us to an orchard between a barn and a farm building. Here silence was interrupted all the time by explosions and gun fire. On the edge of the grave of the victims small trees were planted. The barn was partially burnt down; the rain probably extinguished the flames. The farm itself was standing intact; but behind us were new houses completely burnt out. Mattresses and divans were heaped against the barn's wall and ammunition cartridges were scattered all round. Then we were ordered to level the ground on the grave and immediately started shovelling and digging. Others began to burn the bloodstained mattresses: the ground was saturated with blood. The SS guard left us and we were watched by a gendarme. This enabled us to look around: on one side lay a wheelbarrow originally used for dung. It was red with blood, grey with scattered brains, loaded with bones and entrails. In two places we found holes in the ground: they marked the position of two light machine guns. And all round gun and revolver cartridges. As far as eyes could reach were empty bottles of rum, cognac and other liquors, and wine – together with spectacles, food rations, buttons and caps. The SS man, Wostrel, came up to us. Another SS man brought bottles of beer. We were ordered to dig another hole and bury there all the human remains lying about. I started digging this hole myself to save my comrades the terrible sight. I collected all the human remains and threw them in the hole: I found a cap in which there was a forehead with brains stuck to it – the work of a machine gun. I collected and threw into the hole other pieces of brain, bones, entrails and bloody soil . . . tickets, buttons, cuff links, glasses, Sokol cards, pencils. The [Czech] gendarme who guarded us stood all the time near the farm and looked rather stunned into the distance. Between the farm and the barn stood a perambulator and a toy; when our driver came back, he loaded them on our lorry. Then we could fetch our food from the cellar. But I was told to be careful with the food, for the cellar was inhabited by evil men and they could have poisoned it . . . I took the hint and refused to eat it; my companions too. We went on working in the orchard, with Wostrel shouting at us to work harder. Other SS men, SA and *Schutzpolizie* men ran up and down through the orchard. Then an explosion shattered the silence: the church and the houses round it were swallowed up in dust. The church tower was blown up, but would not come down. The SS men were bored and started shooting pigeons scared by the explosion and flying about madly. Others shot at howling dogs and suddenly the village was full of laughter. Then another explosion interrupted the merrymaking: but the tower again refused to tumble down. We were finishing our levelling task; only dried soil marked the mass grave, the last resting place of the unfortunate victims. We found an iron cross, probably from one of the farms, and placed it lying on the grave. All the time we heard explosions, saw flames and smelt burning houses and smoke. . . not far from us we heard shouting and orders: the labour unit was completing the destruction. All round us a desert: stones, bricks and broken bits, pots, earthenware utensils, destroyed agricultural machinery, burning cars, furniture and pictures.'

When this Jewish commando was taken back to Terezín, Lidice lay in ruin, but Hitler still insisted that it should be levelled to the ground. This task was confined to the *Reichsarbeitsdienst* (Reich Labour Service) which, as a German organisation, could only be ordered to work at Lidice by Frank. On his orders two units of the labour service arrived at Lidice on 11th June. Though the village had been set on fire the day before, it burned throughout the following day. The labour units began to use explosives to shatter the burnt out houses: other SS and army units were also helping with the task of destruction. The SS groups destroyed thirteen buildings, the labour service thirty and army sappers eighty-three. The plan for systematic destruction was very thorough; it was conceived only on 18th June, but went into the minutest details. Calculations were worked out as to the number of labour days needed for the destruction; some 84,000 metres of soil and ruins had to be moved and levelled out; small quarries had to be filled as well as the brook which flowed through the centre of the village past the church. It was a difficult technical task to divert the brook, build a new road, cut down the trees and then cover the whole area with arable soil which could be planted with grain so as to obliterate every trace of the village. In the first days the village was cleared of all things that could be used elsewhere. Then the actual destruction by explosives was started: 140,000 crowns were discovered in the ruins of the houses. However, the labour service was not happy about the operation and demanded reinforcements. Politically the destruction of Lidice proved unattractive even to the German Service and Frank found himself in the rôle of supplicant, in order to complete its obliteration from the map. On 22nd

In order to remove all traces of the village new roads were built, brooks diverted and fields and grazing ground for sheep created over the site

K Čurda of 'Out Distance' Commando who betrayed the Resistance to the Gestapo

June he sent the Labour Service chief, Hierl, a highly significant letter: 'During the investigations into the assassination of the SS-Obergruppen-führer and General of the Police, Heydrich, it was discovered that the village of Lidice near Kladno was a hideout for English-paid parachutist-agents. They hid there repeatedly without ever being denounced by the local inhabitants or the council. It was the Führer's decision to level it to the ground. Men were shot, women taken to a concentration camp and children detailed for special education. Work on the obliteration of the village is currently in progress. After an interview with the Labour Service chief, Commichau, I would like to ask you to despatch two more Labour Service units in the Protectorate for this work . . . The obliteration of the village is a political measure of top significance, for it makes it absolutely clear to the Czechs that the Reich will never permit the existence of any centre of resistance even in the remotest corner of the Protectorate. This measure has impressed the Czech population in a corresponding manner. But to prolong this effect the village must be really levelled to the ground. Frank.'

After this urgent appeal, Hierl allowed two of his units stationed in Moravia to be transferred to Lidice, but they seemed to be as dissatisfied with the work as those from Bohemia and on 29th June Hierl urged Frank to find more suitable units for this type of work. Despite brave words, Commichau's reports to Hierl showed clearly that the young men of the service found the task distasteful: among many disagreeable duties they had to destroy the cemetery, sixty tombs, 140 family graves and 200 individual graves. After three weeks of blasting the village to smithereens the young men from Thuringia, who failed to see the political significance of this destruction, felt lonely and isolated. They had no idea of historical and national differences between them and the local Czechs. They asked to be allowed to go to Prague on a cultural excursion, but no one wanted to pay for it and the young Germans had to continue their hard labour to the bitter end without ever finding out about the historical and cultural differences between the two nations.

Even before the Labour Service commenced work on the clearing of the ruined Lidice houses, other protracted negotiations were undertaken. The labourers asked for new quarters and were given a manor house at Buštěhrad, then Czech school buildings at Hřebenec and Kladno. Engineers worked out a conversion plan: the southern part of Lidice was to be turned into grazing ground for sheep and the rest turned into fields. The roads and paths leading to and through the village were to be diverted and rebuilt so as to make the identification of the old site impossible. Prague officials then decided that the technical equipment for this work as well as the finance for the planned conversion would be supplied by the Czechs themselves. Czech builders had to produce the equipment and the Czech Agricultural Office (under German administration) took charge of finances. Between June and October

114

St Cyril and Methodius Church in Prague hid the parachutists

this highly technical operation was carried out and financed by the Czechs: it cost them some 200,000 DM (three million crowns). In the end the reluctant Labour Service executed all the work required of it.

In March 1943 two additional German units were transferred to Lidice to speed up matters. They obviously used Lidice as a training ground and built a centre for themselves and barracks nearby at Veleslavín with stone and marble from the cemetery. With all their efficiency and thoroughness the Germans, nevertheless, failed to obliterate Lidice permanently. They somehow forgot that Czech agricultural workers were able to observe their operation. After the war, under their guidance, the mass grave, the cemetery and indeed the whole village were easily uncovered and restored.

Even with the destruction of the village the persecution was not complete. On 14th November 1942 the Acting-Protector, Daluege, contrived a further punishment. He issued a decree by which all the property of all the Lidice citizens, as well as that of the commune, became the property of the Reich. Subsequently, the Prague Gestapo issued an administrative instruction by which the district court at Unhošt confiscated the property of 198 persons connected – even if only remotely – with Lidice. The property was then legally transferred to the Reich. Thus, while the village had long since ceased to exist *de facto*, legal transactions continued until late in 1943.

All the Germans concerned in the decision to destroy Lidice and in the destruction itself, claimed after the war that they were convinced that the village was a nest of saboteurs and agents and that Hitler had therefore decided to make an example of it. But the persecutions continued even after it had become quite clear that the

German troops surround the church

assassins had been traced and killed in a pitched battle. It was also established that, apart from possessing addresses of Lidice people, no parachutist from the underground movement ever made use of the village as a hiding place. Nonetheless, the village was destroyed and its inhabitants needlessly massacred. It seems therefore clear that the Lidice atrocities were committed as part of a deliberate German policy of terrorising the Czechs into submission, or even possibly applying to them the same 'final solution' as to the Jews.

It is a bitter paradox that while the tragedy of Lidice was being played out, the denouncement of the assassination was imminent. On 14th June 1942 a letter from K Čurda was delivered at the Czech gendarmerie station at Benešov. Čurda was a member of the commando 'Out Distance' hiding in southern Bohemia. During the hunt for Heydrich's assassins his morale began to crack, for he was hiding at his mother's house. After the announcement of the terrible punishment meted out to Lidice he sent off his letter: 'Stop the investigation of Heydrich's assassination, stop the arrests and executions: the assassins are Gabčík from Slovakia and Jan Kubiš, whose brother is a publican in Moravia.' The letter was unsigned and the Czech gendarmes suitably delayed its delivery to the Gestapo. Čurda, however, became frantic with fear and on 16th June 1942 he travelled to Prague and surrendered himself to the Gestapo. He was immediately interrogated but the Gestapo did not believe him. He was beaten up and assaulted, but persisted with his story. The Gestapo could not understand why Čurda did not give

himself up earlier and why he did it in an anonymous letter. The interrogation dragged on all afternoon and night and ended in the morning of 17th June. Čurda betrayed his commando as well as all he knew about the Resistance. He identified the pistols and other objects found on the spot of the assassination. He betrayed all the persons he knew were helping the parachutists in Prague and Bohemia. But he did not know of the actual hiding places, for he had been out of touch for some time.

Throughout 17th June the Gestapo checked Čurda's tale and operated a wave of arrests. One young man, implicated in the parachutist affair, told the Gestapo, after suitable maltreatment, that all the parachutists were hidden in the crypt of St Cyril and Methodius' church in Prague. It was hastily decided to arrest the parachutists immediately, before they could be warned. At 4.15am on 18th June SS units surrounded the church and blocked all the approaches to it. Some 360 SS men took part in the operation: one heavy machine gun was placed on the roof of the grammar school dominating the church. On the opposite side in another school building was placed a second gun. All inhabitants of the houses near the church were driven out and the priests serving the orthodox church, Petřek and Cikl, were arrested. The SS-*Sturmführer* Pannwitz was in charge of the operation and his orders were to capture the parachutists alive. Father Cikl was forced to unlock the church while another group of Gestapo men broke into the parish office on the opposite side of the church. Seven parachutists, under Lieutenant Opálka's command (the three NCOs involved in the assassination, Valčík, Gabčík and Kubiš, together with the reserve commando, Švarc, Bublík and Hrubý) were hidden in the church waiting for the Germans. That night Opálka, Kubiš and Švarc were on guard in excellent positions on the elevated choir gallery, from which they could control the church entrance as well as see outside into the streets. The others slept in the crypt underground, but at dawn they were alerted when their comrades noticed the Germans arriving. The battle was joined as soon as the Gestapo assistants tried to enter the nave. Lieutenant Opálka fired first and hit one of the Gestapo secretaries. It became clear that the Czechoslovak parachutists would not be taken alive.

As this was going to be a real battle the Gestapo men were withdrawn and their places taken by the SS men of the élite battalion stationed in Prague. They formed themselves into assault groups and supported by the two heavy machine guns which were firing into the church through the windows, tried to storm the nave. The machine gun fire pinned the parachutists down, but they resisted successfully the waves of assaults with concentrated gun fire and hand grenades. After a long combat several SS men succeeded in getting through the nave onto the steps leading towards the choir and galleries. But when two of the SS infiltrators tried to storm the choir from the steps, they were shot down. Nevertheless it was obvious that the three parachutists would only be able to defend themselves and the entrance to their comrades' hideout as long as their ammunition and grenades lasted. The end came after almost three hours of fierce combat. While preparing for another assault, the SS men heard three shots and then stormed the choir and galleries without resistance. The three parachutists fought to their last bullet which was reserved for themselves. Not only were they not taken alive, but the whole operation was now out of gear. Čurda had to be brought from the Gestapo Headquarters to identify the dead. He confirmed that the dead Kubič was one of the assassins.

At 7 am Staatssekretär Frank arrived in person to supervise the operation, this time against the crypt.

The Prague fire brigade prepare to flood the crypt

At first his orders were to try to persuade the trapped parachutists to surrender. He badly wanted the two surviving assassins alive; he wanted to stage a monster trial and massacre every single person connected with them. The Gestapo interpreter, Schwertner, appealed to the parachutists through a small window leading into the crypt from the street. But his cries 'Surrender. Nothing will happen to you', were simply ignored. Then the Gestapo forced Čurda to appeal to his former companions in arms: 'Comrades, surrender! It makes no sense. Surrender your arms and nothing will happen to you. Nothing happened to me . . . Karel Čurda.' His former friends and comrades answered the traitor with gunfire: Frank would have to use other means to take them alive.

The SS troops were ordered to throw tear gas grenades into the crypt through the same small windows which had been used for appeals. The tear gas had no effect on the parachutists, for the crypt was too large and could not be saturated. Moreover the besieged picked up a number of grenades and threw them back into the street. After a while the SS were forced to use gasmasks, while the men in the crypt remained unaffected. Frank then struck on the idea of flooding them from the street: when their ammunition ran out, the SS would take the crypt by assault and capture the men inside alive.

The Prague fire brigade was called, but again the parachutists resisted most successfully; they cut the water pipe and diverted the water elsewhere. At this stage the Germans finally realised the size of the crypt and its possible connection with the nearby Vltava river; they stopped their effort. Then they tried to use demolition equipment to blast a hole into the crypt, but this manoeuvre also

Unsuccessful attempt to flood out the fugitives; they either cut the pipes or diverted the water

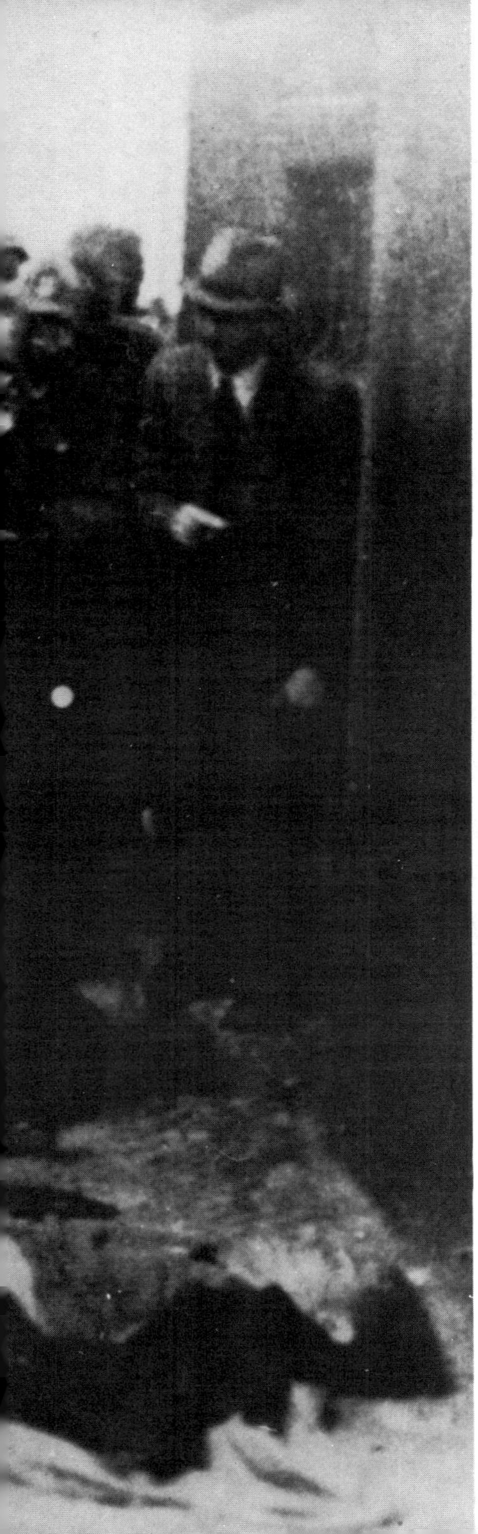

proved impractical. They would have to blow up the church and the houses around before getting anywhere near the hideout. Finally the entrance to the crypt inside the church was discovered: the SS troops would have to use this narrow opening covered by a stone slab in the floor, to break in.

Machine gun and cannon fire was concentrated on the narrow window from the street to cover SS volunteers who were lowered into the dark hole leading into the crypt. The first SS man had his legs shot through as soon as the parachutists caught sight of them. He had to be pulled up again and the disappointed SS began to throw bombs and hand grenades galore into the hole. Finally it was decided to use ladders and after a long shooting match six of them managed to get into the crypt intact. They engaged the defenders in more firing while reinforcements began to flood the crypt. The parachutists' position now was exactly the same as that of their guards: they could only resist until they ran out of ammunition. Two more SS men were seriously wounded before four shots rang out followed by silence. The four parachutists committed suicide with their last bullets. Čurda again identified the bodies, among them those of Gabčík and Valčík. Frank and the Gestapo knew full well that Heydrich's assassination was finally avenged and on 18th June 1942 in the evening the Czech Radio officially broadcast that the investigation of the assassination of SS *Obergruppenführer* Heydrich had been successfully concluded. But possibly because the assassins escaped the tender mercy of German justice, retaliatory actions against the Czechs continued.

On 24th June, another small hamlet, Ležáky, in eastern Bohemia, was surrounded and destroyed. The official announcement was: 'All the adults

The end at last : after the four commandos have committed suicide they are laid out for identification

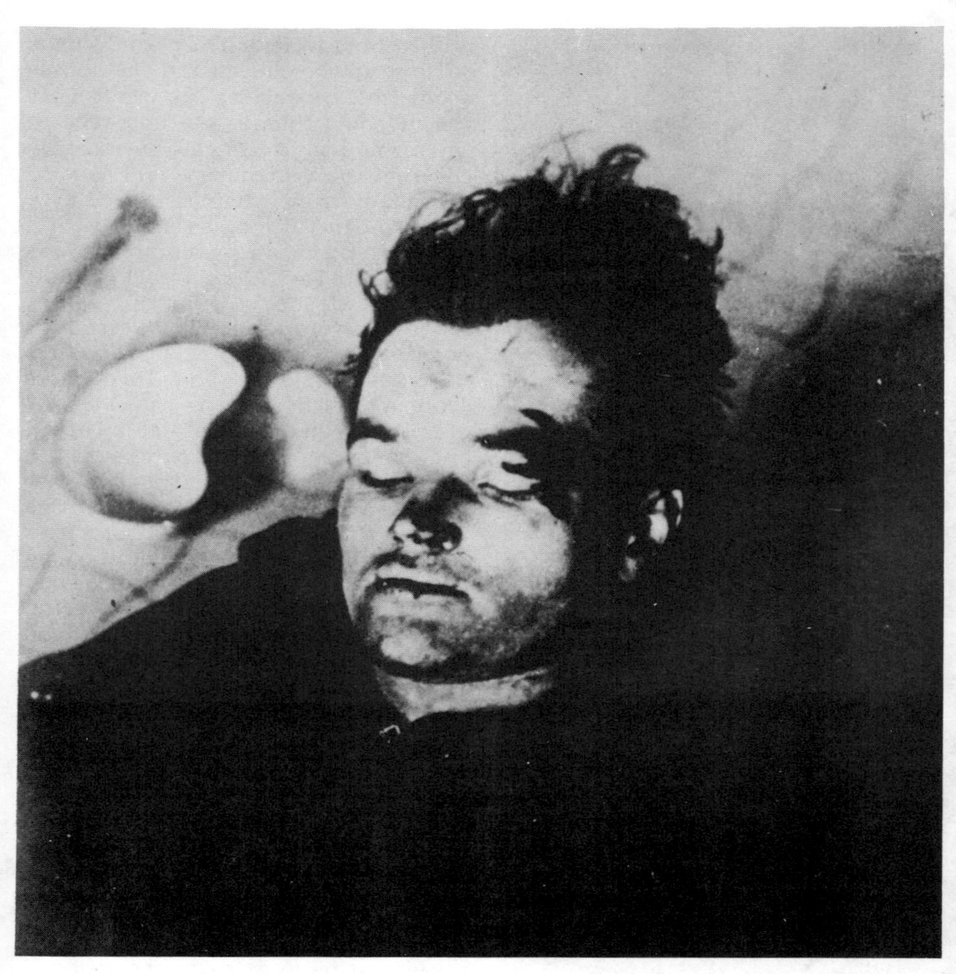

were executed by shooting and the hamlet levelled to the ground. The inhabitants (thirty-four men and women) hid the parachutists-agents who were involved in the assassination of SS-*Obergruppenführer* Heydrich . . . the Czech gendarme responsible for the hamlet who proved to be an accessory committed suicide.' Though the operation was on a smaller scale than that at Lidice, its purpose was similar: to terrorise the Czechs into submission, by making the whole commune responsible for the action of two individuals unconnected with it. The Germans also planned to destroy another village, Bernartice, in

Above: Josef Gabčík after the siege at the church. *Right:* Jan Kubiš committed suicide rather than be captured

southern Bohemia, where they executed twenty-two citizens. Several parachutists found safe hiding places in thé llage and two were captured and executed.

The final stage of the assassination tragedy was played out shortly afterwards. Čurda had surrendered himself and betrayed his comrades because he was morally shattered by the brutality of German retaliations. He wanted to stop the carnage. His friends of 'Anthropoid' were also appalled by the

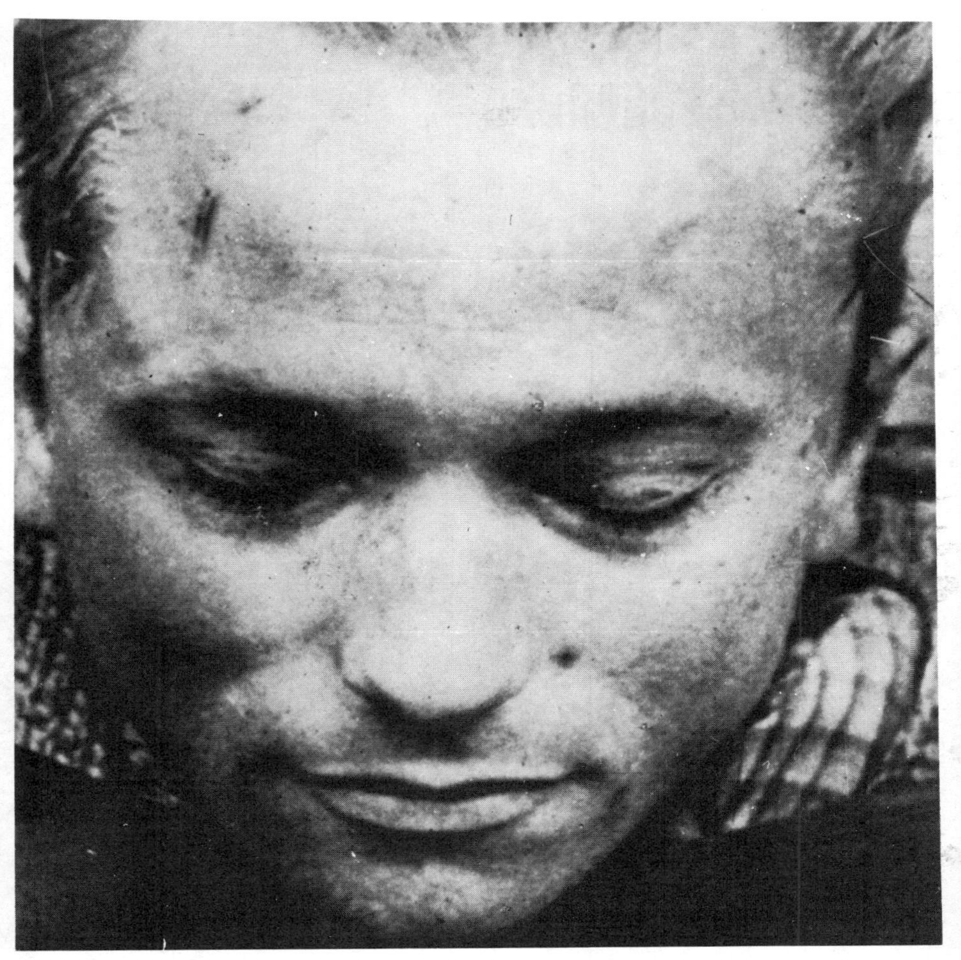

human sacrifice stemming from their deed: they thought of penetrating to the collaborationist minister, Moravec, declaring themselves the assassins, killing the minister and themselves afterwards. However, Lieutenant Opálka put a stop to these fantastic plans, for they would have stopped nothing, as Čurda's action proved. The Gestapo now began to root out the families of all parachutists. All the relations of Kubiš and Valčík were arrested and sent to the concentration camp at Terezín. The Gestapo were exceedingly thorough: everyone by those names, whether related or not, was taken into custody. Paradoxically it could not arrest and exterminate the Gabčíks, for Staff Sergeant Gabčík was a Slovak and Slovakia could resist such encroachments of the Gestapo. On 23rd October 1942 some 250 of them were herded into train carriages and transported to Mauthausen where they were all gassed.

For unknown reasons the operation against Bernartice was never carried out. It is possible that the Germans found out that such terror reprisals were counterproductive: they made the Czechs determined to resist to the death.

Aftermath

The political consequences of Heydrich's assassination and subsequent German persecutions and repressions were internally far-reaching, and in the international sphere, momentous. Internally, President Hácha and the Czech government in Prague not only had to 'apologise' to the Germans, but in order to preserve their own lives, had to disown the emigré movement. The Czech ministers rushed to the hospital where Heydrich was treated and humbly waited for the news in an ante-room. Two days later, President Hácha and the government were received by Frank and given his terms for expiation. On 30th May 1942 the President addressed the nation by radio and accused Beneš and his emigré group of being the cause of all the repressive measures taken by the Germans against the Czechs. He now openly disavowed the emigrés accusing them of being hired agents of foreign powers engaged in the struggle against their own people. The Czech government backed up the President and raised by 10,000,000 crowns the German reward destined for anyone who would lead the authorities to the assassins. President Hácha also asked the Czechs to do their utmost to help the Germans catch the parachutists. In addition, the Czech government allowed the gendarmerie to take part in German repressions and reprisals,

A little girl sits on the stump of the cherry-tree which stood in the school yard at Lidice

President Hácha is received by Neurath and Frank

albeit only in minor duties such as guarding and patrolling.

On 31st May the only truly collaborationist minister, Moravec, spoke to the Czechs on the radio to announce the end of the 'passive era' and the beginning of open collaboration with the Nazi Reich: 'I declare in the name of the Czech government and the nation that henceforth a merciless struggle will be waged against all Czechs who disobey their legal government and their President. The Czech government will put at the disposal of the Reich all its means for the liquidation of the enemy element so that the fifth column is destroyed and peace and order restored. It is clear that Beneš's criminal Jewish clique, when it planned the assassination of the Acting Protector, was quite indifferent to the bloodshed it would cause in the Czech provinces. The BBC's broadcasts only confirm this and in any case

by their inflammatory tone only increase Czech sacrifices...'

In fact the Heydrich affair enmeshed the Czech government so deeply in German misdeeds that no minister or politician could hope to escape responsibility for German crimes and atrocities after the war. Henceforth, there was no alternative but collaboration with the Germans or extinction.

The assassination was an evident attempt at discrediting the loyal Czechs in German eyes. From May 1942 all relations with the emigrés were severed and as a consequence the Czech government at home became absolutely dependent on the Germans. For the rest of the war the President and the government became undignified tools in the hands of their 'protectors'.

On the other hand, the open break between the home government and the emigré movement resulted in the full restoration of political prestige and leadership to President Beneš. When the phase of passive resistance

VERLAUTBARUNG.

Am 27. Mai 1942 wurde in Prag auf den Stellvertretenden Reichsprotektor ᛋᛋ-Obergruppenführer und General der Polizei Heydrich ein Attentat verübt.

Für die Ergreifung der Täter hat bereits der Höhere ᛋᛋ- und Polizeiführer beim Reichsprotektor in Böhmen und Mähren am 27. Mai 1942 eine Belohnung von 10,000.000 K ausgesetzt.

Die Regierung des Protektorates Böhmen und Mähren setzt eine

Belohnung von weiteren

10,000.000 K

für die Ergreifung der Täter aus.

Diese ausgeschriebene Belohnung zahlt die Regierung des Protektorates Böhmen und Mähren bar und ohne Abzüge demjenigen aus, der die Täter ergreift, oder dem, dessen Angaben zur Ergreifung der Täter führen.

Allen Personen wird auf Wunsch eine streng vertrauliche Behandlung ihrer Angaben zugesichert.

Die Regierung des Protektorats Böhmen und Mähren.

Prag, am 30. Mai 1942.

Der Vorsitzende der Regierung:
Dr. J. Krejčí m. p.
Der Minister des Innern:
Bienert m. p.

VYHLÁŠKA.

Dne 27. května 1942 byl v Praze spáchán atentát na Zastupujícího říšského protektora ᛋᛋ-Obergruppenführera generála policie Heydricha.

Na dopadení pachatelů vypsal již Vyšší vedoucí ᛋᛋ a policie u Říšského protektora v Čechách a na Moravě dne 27. května 1942 odměnu 10,000.000 K.

Vláda Protektorátu Čechy a Morava vypisuje na dopadení pachatelů

odměnu dalších

10,000.000 K

Vypsanou odměnu vyplatí vláda Protektorátu Čechy a Morava hotově a beze srážky tomu, kdo pachatele dopadne, nebo tomu, jehož údaje povedou k dopadení pachatelů.

Všem osobám se zaručuje, že jejich údaje na přání budou pokládány za přísně důvěrné.

Vláda Protektorátu Čechy a Morava.

Praha, dne 30. května 1942.

Předseda vlády
Dr. J. Krejčí v. r.
Ministr vnitra
Bienert v. r.

Dr Beneš, now recognised as leader of Czechoslovakia, inspects Czech airmen in England

ended, the Germans had to be fought, by all means possible, because it was now apparent that they were bent on destroying the Czechs. Dr Beneš now assumed the moral leadership of the Czechs at home and abroad and all his claims, constitutional or otherwise, were fully recognised. He was no longer the political leader who, when his policies misfired, resigned and left his country in the lurch: he was reinstated and once again recognised as leader. Thus the Heydrich assassination and ·the tragedy of Lidice rehabilitated Beneš politically in the eyes of the Czech nation. Even more important, it also convinced the Allies, and above all the British, that he was the real leader of the Czechs, not a self-appointed usurper.

Since so many Czechs were willing to sacrifice their lives for his movement, his leadership became indisputable in British eyes. Perhaps not entirely by chance, President Beneš was at the time conducting important negotiations with the British government: he wanted definite recognition for himself, his movement and Czechoslovakia itself, with all that it implied. The Allies, Britain and France, were to acknowledge that Czechoslovakia was destroyed, and take full responsibility for it. The Munich agreement meant the end of Czechoslovakia and of President Beneš. It therefore had to be repudiated. Great Britain had already refused to declare the Munich agreement invalid, but now President Beneš renewed his efforts. Tactically on 9th June 1942, he obtained the USSR's support for the renewed offensive against Munich. Molotov, the Soviet

Beneš inspects Czech army troops in
Britain

Molotov, Soviet Foreign Minister, refused to recognise the Munich agreement

Foreign Minister, who was at the time in London, declared publicly that the USSR had not only refused to be a party in the negotiation but had also refused to recognise the agreement as such. Despite this Soviet support, or perhaps because of it, the British proved unyielding. Throughout June Beneš pressed Eden, the Foreign Secretary, to change the British decision on the treaty, but failed to obtain a favourable response. Eden also disapproved of another Czech demand, namely that the Sudeten Germans who were held as primarily responsible for the destruction of Czechoslovakia, should be resettled in Germany. But already on 24th June, when Beneš had another talk with Eden, it became clear that British attitudes were changing. The impact of the massacre at Lidice and the repression of the Czechs in general proved decisive: on 7th July 1942 Eden informed Beneš that he and his colleagues agreed with the principle of transfer of the Sudeten Germans from Czechoslovakia. The British had be-become vividly aware that after Lidice it would be very difficult for the Czechs to live peacefully side by side with Sudeten Germans.

Finally on 5th August 1942 the British Government, with the Lidice tragedy still fresh in their minds, solemnly repudiated the Munich agreement and the developments resulting from it: the frontier adjustments and population transfers were declared invalid and Czechoslovakia was recognised in its pre-Munich form.

On 29th September 1942 the Free French government under de Gaulle joined the British in the repudiation of the agreement. Thus Dr Beneš at last crowned with success his long struggle for the international re-establishment of Czechoslovakia and of himself as President. It was a great personal victory, but also an immense political gain for his emigré government. The Czechoslovak resistance movement in exile benefited from the aftermath of the Lidice tragedy even more decisively. The doubtful collection of quarrelling politicians was recognised as the real and representative government of the renewed Czechoslovakia and a war ally. Its war aims and demands were recognised by the other Allies; it was also empowered to negotiate or renegotiate treaties and alliances. Its decisions concerning its armies abroad and the plans for the future arrangements at home were respected and backed by the Allies. The most far-reaching decision affecting most fundamentally the future internal situation in Czechoslovakia, i.e. the transfer of Sudeten Germans to Germany, could only have been taken in the post-Lidice days. German atrocities finally convinced world public opinion that it would be impossible for the Czechs to live together with the German minority. Even the United States of America with its own large German minority, found it impossible to oppose this proposed solution. American political leaders and public opinion were not only favourable to the Czechs, but even tried to draw a philosophy of war from this tragedy (after all the world did not yet know the truth about concentration camps and other greater atrocities). As early as 13th June 1942 the American Sec-

Above : Beneš with Anthony Eden. *Below :* Czech recruits are paraded in Britain

CBS
CBS

retary of the Navy, F Knox, declared in Boston that 'if future generations asked us what we were fighting for in this war, we should tell them the story of Lidice.' In fact, the Americans were the most outraged of all, and the next day the Secretary of State, Cordell Hull, put on record the shock reports of the events and the *Manchester Guardian* added a poem called *Lidice*.

Protest campaigns were started spontaneously and more permanent movements began to be organised. On 23rd June 1942 W J Browne, MP issued a warning to the Germans on the BBC in the most emotional terms: 'Think of my words, Chancellor Hitler. Do think of them, Himmler. Bear them in mind, Göring, Goebbels, Ribbentrop and all others. The day of reckoning is coming nearer every day, wherever you may be. The steps of the Great Avenger sound clearer every night. You cannot run away and hide . . . heed this voice of England. We are not unarmed fighting a defensive battle to protect our women and children from the fate of the Lidice victims . . . we are the tools of the despised Providence . . . and you will be destroyed.'

Since Lidice was a humble village, where many miners lived, the National Union of Miners took up its cause as a matter of course. Immediately it organised a protest meeting in Stoke-on-Trent presided over by the local member of Parliament, Dr Barnett Stross. President Beneš as well as the Prime Ministers of Belgium, Holland, France, Jugoslavia, Norway, Poland and Greece attended this meeting. Commonwealth High Commissioners as well as the Ambassadors of the USA and USSR expressed by their presence their governments' condemnation of German brutality.

Subsequently, the Union passed a resolution which expressed the general feeling of sympathy in the most concrete terms. It proposed to set up a fund of £1,000,000 for a campaign

**American Secretary of the Navy
Frank Knox**

entitled 'Lidice shall live'. This initiative proved most fruitful: under the impact of the tragedy public response was generous. Committees were set up all over the world to collect contributions for the fund. At the same time a committee of architects and consultants was formed to prepare a plan for the post-war reconstruction of the commune of Lidice. The campaign was launched in October 1942 and caught the imagination of all and sundry. Although every contribution was welcome and accepted, the miners' initiative was always stressed and mining trade unions from all over the world contributed most. In a sense the 'Lidice shall live' movement became the expression of international solidarity among the miners. During a ceremony in London, G H Jones, the Secretary of the Union, declared that the aim of the campaign was to show the world that barbarism could never triumph.

The British Ministry of Information decided that a film of the tragedy would not be out of place. The film was shot in Wales in the mining village of Cwmgiedd, and to lend it added authenticity the actors were in fact the miners and their families living in the village. Will Lawther, the miners' leader presented a copy of the film, 'The Silenced Village', to the emigré Czechoslovak miners' leader, J Bečko, during an anniversary celebration in London a year later. Lawther's speech, in which he reminded the world of what happened at Lidice and pleaded for remembrance, was broadcast by the BBC to Czechoslovakia. Lidice anniversaries were celebrated everywhere in Great Britain with much pomp: in bombed-out Bermondsey Minister Jan Masaryk compared the tragedies; V Martinů composed 'Monument-Lidice' for the anniversary; it was broadcast by the BBC Symphony Orchestra. By the time of this anniversary the British-inspired campaign 'Lidice shall live' was spreading all over the world.

With the largest number of Czechs

The Mayor of New York, Fiorello La Guardia, head of the 'Lidice shall live' National Committee,with Beneš

and Slovaks living in the USA, the greatest number of 'Lidice shall live' committees was founded there. The National Committee was headed by the Mayor of New York, Fiorello La Guardia and many other political personalities sat on the committee. On 12th July 1942 Wendell Wilkie addressed a protest gathering at Stern Park Gardens, a small town in Illinois, which was the first of many to change its name to Lidice. Wilkie declared that Lidice in Czechoslovakia was destroyed by barbarians, but it should live in the hearts of all freedom loving people. Many other American communes followed this example. President Roosevelt publicly approved this movement of good will. In his message he said: 'On 10th June 1942 the Nazi government announced its murder of the name Lidice. It was not only the small village that was des-troyed but also the men, who were murdered and the women and children who disappeared in prisons. Lidice should have been blotted out for ever . . . The enlightened citizens of a small American commune took the name of Lidice. Instead of oblivion, as the Germans had wanted, Lidice lives again. In the green valley near the Great Lakes on the Mississipi River the name and village Lidice remind us of the unforgettable tragedy . . .' In October 1942 the model of Lidice was unveiled in the New York City Museum and architects at Columbia University began to plan the reconstruction of the new Lidice after the war. The renaming movement spread all over America: in Mexico, San Jeronimo became Lidice; a suburb of Caracas was named after the village; Havana changed one of its squares into Plaza de Lidice; so did Callao in Peru and Quito in Ecuador, Vino de Mar in Chile and Montevideo in Uruguay. In May 1945 the United States Congress passed a resolution authorising the President, Harry S Truman, to proclaim the 10th June 'Lidice Day'.

In the USSR the communications media were slower in picking up the tragic news of Lidice and commenting on it. Politically the news was unwelcome, for it showed the world that the Czechs were ready for any sacrifice for their 'bourgeois' nationalist movement and leadership in Britain. The communist comments broadcast to Czechoslovakia on 6th July were full of historic imagery, but failed to link the heroic sacrifice with the current struggle waged by the emigrés from Britain against Germany.

Nevertheless the Czechs and Slovaks serving in the Red Army were instantly touched by the tragedy. Their commanding officer, General Svoboda, launched an appeal and protests against the barbaric deed. The Czechoslovaks began to collect money, but not to rebuild Lidice after the war.

Two tanks were purchased with the proceeds and named Lidice and Ležáky to commemorate the hamlet which shared the fate of Lidice. It took some time before the Soviets became aware of the symbolic value of this name and began to enthuse about it. (They also corrected their original misspelling of the village – Libice.) In 1944 Ilya Ehrenburg explained why they were so late: 'There are thousands of such Lidices in our country . . . but it is not by chance that the name Lidice became known all over the world . . . the Czechs, a peaceful nation, now surrounded by the Germans face death daily in their struggle to weaken the enemy . . . but today Czechoslovakia is not far away . . . freedom is coming . . . with it the moment of revenge for Lidice.' It is obvious that the USSR

A meeting at Stern Park Gardens, Illinois, one of the first towns to change its name to Lidice

Mal.
Lidice
310

had too many Lidices at home to worry much about another. To the end the Soviet and the Czechoslovak communists in exile in the Soviet Union were convinced that the events at Lidice were the result of a tremendous political miscalculation by the non-Communist Czechoslovaks. The celebration of Lidice in the USSR and by Soviet communists would come later, after the war, and above all, after Czechoslovakia itself became communist.

It can be seen that as a consequence of Heydrich's assassination and the destruction of Lidice, the Czechoslovak emigré cause was greatly favoured internationally. Lidice was one of the first atrocities committed openly and for the whole world to see. Later on many other destructions and mass shootings took place in Czechoslovakia: at Leskovice twenty-five men, women and children were executed and some 230 houses blown up. At Grun and Klak, two neighbouring hamlets in Slovakia, 336 houses were destroyed and 148 people executed (thirty-two children among them). But these were reprisals for sheltering partisans or resisting German troops. Even the greatest German atrocity, in France at Oradour-sur-Glane, where some 800 people perished in June 1944, did not shock the rest of the world as much as Lidice. Though this village was also destroyed by mistake, and its inhabitants slaughtered in vain, all this was done by enraged SS troops running for their lives. What shocked most at Lidice was the systematic cold-bloodedness of the operation. This fired the world's imagination, and inspired a huge wave of sympathy and goodwill.

The world had come finally to believe that Czechoslovakia was on the side of the Allies, fighting and shedding blood for them in their occupied country. There was no shirking or sitting on the fence: the Czechs pro-

Architects from Columbia University discuss the plans for the new Lidice

Children from San Jeronimo, Mexico.
This village was one of those that
changed its name after Lidice's end

nounced themselves clearly for the Allies. The recognition of this fact was implied in the international recognition of President Beneš and his government as the true representatives of a free Czechoslovakia. The shock of the tragedy drove home to the Allied powers the injustice of their deal with Hitler in Munich and led to its repudiation.

Only in one respect were the effects of Heydrich and Lidice purely negative: the home resistance movement. First of all SOE operations in Czechoslovakia came virtually to an end. The demise of the parachutists directly involved in the attempt has already been outlined; 'Anthropoid', 'Bioscope', 'Outdistance' and one member of the 'Tin' commando were killed: the rest rapidly fell victims to the frantic German hunt and their own collapse of morale. Čurda, who had been so frightened by the carnage resulting from the assassination that he had changed sides, was joined by Gerik. Čurda's revelations led the Gestapo to Pardubice, which was 'Silver A''s operational headquarters. Captain Bartoš's contacts were arrested and during a search of their appartment Bartoš's diaries and codes were found. The Gestapo remained in the flat waiting for Captain Bartoš. He turned up on 21st June 1942, but committed suicide rather than fall into German hands. Because of the codes which the Gestapo had found, some eighty-six persons were arrested in Prague, forty at Pardubice, eleven at Pilsen and four at Lázně Buštěhrad. J Potůček, Bartoš's radio operator, was shot dead by Czech gendarmes shortly afterwards.

Early in July 1942 O Dvořák of 'Steel' commando was shot dead. By the end of the year, out of twenty-six parachutists dropped in Czechoslovakia, fourteen were dead, three were in jail and two had changed sides: only seven

General Ludvík Svoboda, commander of the Czechs and Slovaks serving in the Russian army

were still operating. Rather optimistically, London decided to strengthen these hunted and demoralised resistance fighters and three more commandoes, 'Antimony', 'Iridium' and 'Bronze', were destined for Czechoslovakia. But only 'Antimony' was successfully dropped in October 1942. The end was near for them all. 'Antimony' was trapped in January 1943 and Lieutenant Zázvorka and his radio man, Lieutenant Jasínek, committed suicide. The last member, Sergeant S Srazil, was captured and under duress betrayed people who had helped him, ultimately changing sides.

In March 1943 the commando, 'Intransitive', was betrayed to the Gestapo and its commanding officer, V Kindl, changed sides and denounced his own men: Lukaštík was shot dead, fighting it out with the Gestapo. Lieutenant Cupal of 'Tin' was cornered and committed suicide and his Sergeant Hauptfogel was shot dead while trying to escape from an ambush. Mladý, Commanding Officer of commando 'Embassy', was also cornered and shot dead in a gun fight; J Odstrčil, CO of 'Calcium' was also shot dead by the Germans. In fact by March 1943, all the parachutists involved in the resistance movement in Czechoslovakia was either dead or co-operating with the Germans. In the same month London decided to drop the two commandoes, 'Bronze' and 'Iridium', but they were both shot down over Germany. Thus in 1943 the emigré movement had lost contact with Czechoslovakia, the resistance movement was disorganised and infiltrated by the Gestapo, and operations were no longer possible.

Only in 1944 did London re-establish contact with Czechoslovakia and new commandoes were landed. But these operations, by commandoes 'Calcium', 'Barium', 'Magnesium', 'Sulphur', 'Sodium', 'Aluminium', 'Spelter' and 'Glucinium', were purely Intelligence missions, for there was practically no resistance movement left to co-operate with and lead. Al-

Some of the twenty-five Czechs
executed at Leskovice

Above : View of the burning village of Klak after reprisals by the Germans. *Right :* Severe damage after the sack of Grun by members of the German *Edelweiss* unit. *Below :* The Prague uprising of May 1945

Czech Resistance fighters take part in the spontaneous uprising

Russian troops in Prague, May 1945

Frank on trial in April 1946

though the commandoes dropped in 1944 did co-operate with partisan groups, these were small groups of combatants consisting mainly of escaped prisoners-of-war and Czech deserters, operating in forests and mountains. Politically they were insignificant. Thus the emigré movement lost not only its grip on the resistance movement but also lost control in general. Acts of sabotage against the Germans and even partisan struggle were conducted spontaneously without any overall organisation, and consequently no political benefit could be derived from them. Even the last minute uprising in Prague in May 1945 was a spontaneous act beyond emigré control, and therefore without benefit for the Czechoslovak government in exile.

Without any control over the resistance group and with the Red Army occupying its territory, the future of the emigré Czechoslovak government began to look bleak.

The persecutions following Heydrich's assassination did not destroy the parachutists only: the resistance movement was also mortally struck. The third central committee of the underground communist party was discovered during the intensive hunt for the assassins. The Gestapo showed no mercy towards these Czechs and they were all slaughtered. The central committee was reformed only late in 1944; but the party seems to have had the same ill luck as the non-communists. More communists were caught and killed by the Germans in March 1945; the few survivors, among whom J Smrkovský, the hero of 1968, took an active part in the Prague

uprising in May 1945. The *Obrana národa* and *Vérni züstaneme* which were uncovered before Heydrich's assassination were mercilessly rooted out. The leaders of these two organisations formed the bulk of the mass executions; the rank and file members were sent to concentration camps. The non-communist resistance movement timidly began to renew its organisation late in 1943 and 1944, but its activity never reached the scope and scale of the pre-1942 days. In fact the movement never recovered from the losses and lost overall initiative and leadership in the resistance struggle. In the last months of the war the resistance movement was activated by the left-wing oriented partisan groups, but their political and military significance was limited.

After three years of more or less peaceful coexistence, the assassination of Heydrich was a great divide for Czechoslovakia. Up to 1942, Czech losses arising out of resistance to the Germans were relatively low: however, by the end of the war they amounted to some 250,000. 75,000 Czechs were executed by the Germans (of these 3,649 were communists) and some 127,816 people permanently crippled as a result of imprisonment or ill treatment. German terrorism against the Czech population did not stop; even in the last days of the war the retreating units of the Wehrmacht and the SS committed numerous atrocities. Out of 203 Lidice women only 143 returned 'home' after the war; of 104 children only sixteen were traced and repatriated to Czechoslovakia.

Frank's execution by the Czechs in
1946

Bibliography

Attentat auf den Chef der Sicherheitspolizei und der S.D. Stellvertretenden Reichsprotektor SS-Obergruppenführer Heydrich, RSHA 5 August 1942, YIVO Institute for Jewish Research, New York
Lidice. Čin krvavého teroru i proušení zákonů a základních lidských práv, Ministry of the Interior, Prague, 1945
Lidice, Prague, 1957
Zpoved K H Franka, Prague, 1946
C Amort, I M Jedlička, *Hledá se zradce X*, Prague, 1968
John Bradley, *Czechoslovakia: A History*, Edinburgh, 1971
T Brod, J Čejka, *Na západní fronté*, Prague, 1965
J Doležal, *Jediná cesta*, Prague, 1966
D Hamšík, J Pražák, *Bomba pro Heydricha*, Prague, 1965
V. Král, *Otázky hospodářského a sociálního vyvoje v ceskych zemích* 1938-1945, 3 vols, Prague, 1957-59
B Laštovička, *V Londyne za války*, Prague, 1960